**Required Reading Range
Course Reader**

academia

An AVA Book
Published by AVA Publishing SA
Rue des Fontenailles 16
Case Postale
1000 Lausanne 6
Switzerland
Tel: +41 786 005 109
Email: enquiries@avabooks.com

Distributed by Thames & Hudson (ex-North America)
181a High Holborn
London WC1V 7QX
United Kingdom
Tel: +44 20 7845 5000
Fax: +44 20 7845 5055
Email: sales@thameshudson.co.uk
www.thamesandhudson.com

Distributed in the USA & Canada by:
Ingram Publisher Services Inc.
1 Ingram Blvd.
La Vergne TN 37086
USA
Tel: +1 866 400 5351
Fax: +1 800 838 1149
Email: customer.service@ingrampublisherservices.com

English Language Support Office
AVA Publishing (UK) Ltd.
Tel: +44 1903 204 455
Email: enquiries@avabooks.com

© AVA Publishing SA 2011

ISBN 978-2-940411-41-2

Library of Congress Cataloging-in-Publication Data
Ambrose, Gavin.
Packaging the Brand: Exploring the relationship between packaging design and brand identity /
Gavin Ambrose p. cm.
Includes bibliographical references and index.
ISBN: 9782940411412 (pbk.:alk.paper)
eISBN: 9782940439799
1. Packaging--Design. 2. Packaging--Design--Study and teaching.
TS195.4 .A537 2011

10 9 8 7 6 5 4 3 2 1

Design by Gavin Ambrose

Production by AVA Book Production Pte. Ltd., Singapore
Tel: +65 6334 8173
Fax: +65 6259 9830
Email: production@avabooks.com.sg

Printed in China

Packaging the Brand

Required Reading Range
Course Reader

**Gavin Ambrose
Paul Harris**

**The relationship between
packaging design and brand
identity**

Ethical:
aware-
ness/
reflect-
ion/
debate

**a
va
academia**

Contents

1

The 'packaged' brand   10

2

Research and concept   52

3

Design approaches 94

4

Form and elements 134

5

The future 180

Introduction

Welcome to *Packaging the Brand*, a book that will introduce you to the design and creation of packaging as it forms part of the product branding process. This book aims to explore the many different ways by which brands come to be packaged and to consider the design processes that are undertaken to achieve this. Packaging and branding are sometimes treated as separate disciplines, with packaging being primarily about how a product is protected and contained, and branding about how a product's characteristics will be communicated to consumers. Yet, if we take a closer look, it quickly becomes obvious that these disciplines are in fact very much entwined.

Packaging and its design has come to play an increasingly prominent role in the branding exercise as the scope and extent of branding has grown; it is no longer merely concerned with the need to contain and protect a product. Packaging has become more sophisticated as a result and today plays a key part in the brand communication process; for many product groups, packaging has become a fundamental element of the brand statement, if not the defining one.

Packaging the Brand will provide you with a comprehensive insight into the packaging design process, from initial research to developing brand concepts and the brand message, through to execution of the design idea and finally, production of the packaging itself. The book uses real examples commissioned from contemporary design studios to give you valuable insights into how the exciting process of packaging design takes place in practice and to show you the social and cultural variations that exist around the world.

How to get the most out of this book

Case studies
Each chapter features a case study that directly explores the main chapter content in more detail, with precise reference to a real-life example.

Key texts
Each chapter of this book begins with an essay or extract of critical writing from the broader spectrum of design thinking. This vignette is meant to function as an *agent provocateur*, to present a point of view that is deliberately provocative in nature. It provides a stance for you to react to and is intended to challenge our general perceptions of design, specifically those which relate to packaging design.

Navigation
A simple breadcrumb navigation bar allows you to see where you are in the book and to find out what content is coming up next.

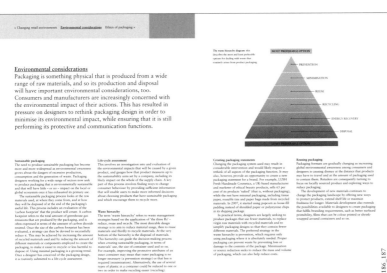

Features
Each spread features design elements that include diagrams, quotations and examples of contemporary design work.

Student exercises
Each chapter ends with a student exercise that draws upon some of the featured contemporary design work from within that chapter.

The 'packaged' brand

Physical products require packaging to protect them from damage and to present both the product and its brand attractively to a target group of consumers. Packaging provides a surface upon which to communicate information about the product and the brand, and as such, it is an essential element of product branding. Through the use of text, images and other communication devices, packaging can articulate the attributes and benefits of a product to consumers. Packaging also works to convey the brand characteristics that will position it within the minds of consumers and that will ultimately differentiate it from its competitors.

Packaging is often the first point of contact that a consumer has with a brand, so it is hugely important that it initially draws their attention and also quickly conveys the messages that both present and support the brand. Communicating a brand message extends beyond the information and visual content of packaging. The physical materials used for packaging products also importantly contribute to the overall brand statement projected. A brand cannot be positioned as a high quality or luxury product if its packaging is fragile and low quality. There has to be a direct correlation between the packaging's physical attributes and the messages that the brand seeks to project.

This chapter will explore some general concepts about packaging and branding, and look at the dynamic relationship between them.

'You have two goblets before you. One is of solid gold, wrought in the most exquisite patterns. The other is of crystal-clear glass, thin as a bubble, and as transparent. Pour and drink; and according to your choice of goblet, I shall know whether or not you are a connoisseur of wine. For if you have no feelings about wine one way or the other, you will want the sensation of drinking the stuff out of a vessel that may have cost thousands of pounds; but if you are a member of that vanishing tribe, the amateurs of fine vintages, you will choose the crystal, because everything about it is calculated to reveal rather than to hide the beautiful thing which it was meant to contain.'

Beatrice Warde, 1932

Key text

The Crystal Goblet

Beatrice Warde

The quotation on the facing page is an excerpt from a speech delivered to the British Typographers Guild in 1932 called 'The Crystal Goblet', or 'Printing Should Be Invisible', by the twentieth-century typographer, Beatrice Warde. Warde's essay questioned whether design's role should be crucially one of embellishment or elaboration, with design adding to a brand or product; or whether design's role should be essentially neutral, like the clear crystal of the glass in the analogy that she uses. This question about the real purpose of design remains a hot topic and presents an interesting debate that can be equally applied to packaging design.

What do we mean by 'packaging design'?
What *is* packaging design? At first, the answer might seem obvious, but this is an overly simplistic question and one that actually has many answers. The answer *you* give will depend on where you work, what you work on, how you approach your work and how you came to be where you are. As with all areas of design, the answer ultimately stems from the project that you are working on; but it also rests with you, the designer.

What then do designers bring to packaging design? To some people, design represents a mental wrestle, an intellectual pursuit that requires the shaping and forming of ideas and concepts. To others, it is about the craft of making something, applying and refining the smallest of details, and the nuances of choice involved. Both approaches are valid and, throughout the history of design, there have been active proponents of each.

Warde challenged whether typography should add to a message or whether it should transparently present it, without further elaboration. The relevance of this analogy to packaging design (or any form of design, be it typography, advertising or graphic design) is clear. Is it our role as designers to add to a design or to be merely neutral messengers of it? Warde's question raises many issues and the answer is far from simple. Indeed, for many people there simply is no single answer.

A piece of packaging is a story that conveys a narrative to an audience. It is more than a mere container adorned with graphics; it is a message, a medium, and a conversation between buyer and seller. Should a designer add to this message or be content to be a neutral conveyor of information?

In a globalised and saturated market, there is often little inherent difference between like-for-like products. The points of difference are slight; it is design that helps us to differentiate one product from another. For many end users, the design and packaging of a product *are* the product and go to make up the distinguishing qualities that enable one product to stand out from the next. It is often while looking at packaging that we make decisions about and form alliances with brands, which can be emotional and long-lasting.

This is arguably the main responsibility of designers; to enrich, inform and entertain, and so make people's experience of products easier. But it is also a designer's responsibility to be truthful in their intentions and accurate in their delivery of them, as they deal not only with design in terms of colours and shapes, but crucially also with users' relationships with brands.

This chapter will raise the following questions:
- What role do designers play in packaging design?
- What moral stance do you take as a designer?
- Is the product or the brand more important?
- What is truth in design?
- What do you as a designer bring to design?

< Key text   **Is packaging branding?**   What is packaging design?>

'Packaging *is* branding'

Richard Gerstman, chairman, Interbrand

Is packaging branding?

It could be argued that packaging is part of the overall graphic communications mix for many brands; and that the brand manifests through advertising, marketing, public relations and online viral communications. As such, packaging becomes merely another way of usefully communicating a brand's values to consumers.

Conversely, it can be argued that a package and a brand are essentially inseparable. Consider, for instance, a can of Coca-Cola: the can is a means to contain liquid, while Coca-Cola (the brand) represents a set of values related to the product. Can the two really be separated or are they inextricably linked? If you separate the brand from its packaging, you are left with the physical packaging (a metal container) and a set of fonts, colours and graphics that constitute its branding. But together they magically form a 'packaged brand', and the product thus gains value.

Creatives have differing opinions about the relationship between branding and packaging. Packaging and branding can be treated as discrete elements, but to most end users, what is important is the point at which these two elements coalesce or successfully combine.

As users, we do not make the conceptual distinctions that designers might. We simply view products as single entities, whether it be a *can* of drink, a *bar* of soap or a *box* of washing powder. Even the way in which we describe or ask for such items incorporates the container it comes packaged in with the product or brand name.

'Packaging and branding are *different*'

Darrel Rhea, CEO, Cheskin

Branded packaging design can take this a step further by creating unique packaging for a brand, in place of the all-too-ubiquitous options typically available, such as the common tin can. In this book, we will explore how branding can be extended through the creation of new packaging shapes, forms and containers, which ultimately help to differentiate a brand.

What does this debate mean for those involved in packaging design? To create truly effective packaged brands, designers need to consider how both packaging *and* the brand can be dovetailed together in a way that mutually and effectively serves both the packaging and branding goals of a product. Branded packaging design creates something greater than the sum of its parts.

Some would argue that packaging *is* branding; that packaging represents the manifestation of the brand and the brand lives through and is enlivened by the packaging. For the end user, packaging is part of a product, from which to gain confidence in and develop loyalty towards the product. To generate such brand loyalty represents the packaging designer's real challenge.

< Is packaging branding? **What is packaging design?** Branding and rebranding >

What is packaging design?

Packaging design is one of the key elements of a marketing strategy for a product as it is the visual face that will be promoted, recognised and sought out by the consumer.

The 'four Ps'

Packaging works within what is known as the marketing mix, a collection of activities to maximise product awareness and sales. The marketing mix comprises the 'four Ps': product, price, promotion and place. Some marketers also talk of a fifth 'P': packaging. *Product* is the combination of physical characteristics and service elements that will meet a customer's needs. *Price* is how much people will pay for the product, hopefully one high enough to cover costs and generate profits; however, there are various pricing strategies depending upon the overall goals of an organisation. *Promotion* is the effort made to raise awareness of a product or service through various activities, such as advertising and sales promotions. Finally, there is *place*, the location where a product will be presented to the consumer, such as a supermarket or a boutique store. The fifth 'P', *packaging*, synthesises the previous four components into the visual 'face' of a brand and brings together the physical characteristics of the product, its pricing strategy (that is, whether it is a premium or cheap product), how it will be promoted and where it will be sold.

Packaging design can thus be viewed in four different ways: as a means of protecting the product (which can form part of the product experience); as a contributor to product cost; as a canvas on which to promote the product's attributes and benefits; and as a dispensing aid in the place of sale and for final consumption.

The 'four Cs'

Some marketers now dismiss the 'four Ps' as being out of date and instead favour use of the 'four Cs', developed by Professor Robert F Lauterborn, a pioneer of Integrated Marketing Communication, and advanced by marketing guru Philip Kotler. Under this scheme, place becomes convenience, price becomes cost to the user, promotion becomes communication or canvas, and product becomes customer needs and wants. This method reflects a more customer-oriented marketing philosophy that emphasises the need for marketing to be focused entirely on the consumer.

Using the Ps and Cs

Packaging design straddles many disciplines; at its core, it is concerned with aligning and unifying the various areas contained within the marketing mix. Use of both the four Ps and four Cs can place packaging design in a wider context; they may additionally be used as a series of questions or reference points that keep the design process focused on reflecting back the consumer's wants and needs. Do I know *who* I am aiming the product and packaging design at? Do I *understand* the product and the target group? Is the design *relevant* to the target group I am aiming at?

The 'four Cs' of packaging design: convenience, cost, communication and customer needs.

Cloud Nine

The design agency Propaganda created the packaging pictured here for Cloud Nine, a new hairstyling-iron brand that aspires to become the market leader. In a sector saturated by brightly coloured and heavily patterned 'limited edition' styling irons, Cloud Nine decided to offer a classic and sophisticated alternative to reinforce the brand message that this is a professional hairstyling tool. The presentation box is 'covered in black buckram with a foil-block silver logo on the front and top. A simple diagonal split on the sides of the hinged lid reveals a flash of cyan, and the box is wrapped in a matt sleeve that protects it from damage and gives full product information,' explains Lee Bennett of Propaganda.

< What is packaging design?   **Branding and rebranding**   Audiences and sectors >

Branding and rebranding

Branding and packaging have a lifecycle, which means there is a need for regular evaluation and alteration in order to maintain a brand, its attributes and personality. When a brand no longer resonates with its target consumers, it is often time to undertake a rebranding of the product or line to correct this.

The new and the old

When undertaking a brand review, the first step is to identify and focus on the attributes that are really important. Often, brand designers try to focus on too many things. Once you have decided on what is important, you can review where the brand sits against its competition. An existing brand will be known in the marketplace and may have both good and bad associations for buyers. A new brand has none of this baggage and represents a clean slate to be positioned before consumers. The designer can construct any narrative they choose for a new brand in order for it to penetrate and successfully compete in an existing market with already well-established brands.

To do this, a new brand often takes a divergent approach from those adopted for similar products, so as to stand out from the competition. If this strategy is successful, it may, over time, become the brand that is copied by its competitors and so will invariably end up lost in a sea of similar designs. A brand redesign or a rebrand can then be undertaken to establish a new point of difference.

Brands for life

National brands, supported by national advertising, can find their way into the national psyche and so become part of everyday folk or popular culture. There are many examples of products that people grew up with and still maintain a nostalgic attachment to throughout adulthood. This is especially the case with food products; every country in the world has numerous national food products that have become an integral part of that country's cultural identity in this way. In the UK, such foods might include Branston Pickle, Marmite, Oxo and Ambrosia Creamed Rice, to name just a few examples. Products that are likely to evoke a similar feeling in the US include Cheez Whiz, Vermont cheddar, Pillsbury baked products and Hershey chocolate. Some national or regional products become so successful over time that they become well known and loved internationally.

Launching a new brand and rebranding

Launching a new brand has specific considerations, such as determining which segment of the market you intend to target. The market segment will inform the communication strategies that need to be adopted in order to communicate to consumers within it. Market segmentation is an activity that seeks to determine how different brands compete on two key competitive characteristics, such as price and quality. Each brand in the market can be plotted on a simple chart displaying these characteristics. This may help indicate where an opportunity or target niche for a new product exists and the combination of characteristics required from it.

Once the target market segment has been identified, a product can be adjusted or formulated to meet the requirements of that segment, such as by increasing or decreasing the quality, or by adapting the mixture of materials to hit a certain price point band. The packaging communication strategies of the competing brands at that positioning point can be analysed and a decision then taken as to whether the new brand will adopt a convergent, divergent or transformation communication strategy. The brand packaging communication will be developed to appeal directly to the consumers in the target market segment.

'The bold single colours help to differentiate the variants and make the product stand out well on the shelf against the kaleidoscope of colour surrounding it. The designs also make the most of the metal substrate and print limitations.'

Kasia Rust – creative director, burst*

Superdrug body sprays

Pictured above is a rebrand created by burst* designer Sophie Mockford, for body sprays for the UK health and beauty shop, Superdrug. Pictured far left is the old can design against the new design (to its right). Notice that the container is physically the same and that only the graphics have changed during the rebrand via use of an illustration by McFaul Studio, with art direction from Kasia Rust, burst*s creative director. The can has essentially been reskinned to update the brand message, a move which successfully improved sales by 350 per cent. The new design presents a bolder graphic solution that is more eye-catching and which more successfully targets the younger, fashion-conscious, trend-led customer that it is designed to appeal to. Notice also that each variant of the design benefits from the use of a shared visual language, and that it is the graphics alone that have created the differences between the products in Superdrug's range.

< Branding and rebranding   **Audiences and sectors**   Purpose and intent >

Audiences and sectors
Packaging design extends beyond creating a container within which to place a product (a task that is relatively straightforward), to produce something that communicates directly to the target audience and so establishes a positive connection. Successful packaging design requires consideration of two main factors in this context: *audiences* and *sectors*.

Audiences
The first step to successful packaging design is to identify the main audience that the design will appeal to. Motivational sales speaker and training consultant Mark Hunter, believes that instead of creating packaging that strives to continually compete for new customers, the focus of packaging designers should really be on the 20 per cent of clients who represent the best customers and therefore the most reliable ongoing opportunity. Hunter posits that there are five main types of shoppers:

1 *Loyal customers,* who represent no more than 20 per cent of the customer base, but who account for more than 50 per cent of sales.

2 *Discount customers,* who shop frequently, but who make decisions based on the size of markdowns.

3 *Impulse customers,* who do not have buying a particular item at the top of their 'to do' list, but who purchase what seems good at the time.

4 *Needs-based customer*s, who go out with a specific intention to buy a particular type of item.

5 *Wandering customers,* who have no specific need or desire in mind, but who rather hope to gain a sense of experience and/or community.

Character profiles
Designing packaging is about more than the finish and graphics of a container. A beautifully created design will be a failure if the message it transmits is not recognised or accepted by the target market. Using floral patterns on male cosmetic products is unlikely to result in success, as they will are likely to conflict with the masculine self-image of the target market. Care does need to be taken to ensure that a suitable message is delivered, which may be harder than you might think. 'Modern packages are inherently bundles of contradictions. They engage us consciously and unconsciously. They are physical structures but at the same time they are very much about illusion. They appeal to our emotions as well as to our reason,' claims writer Randall Frost.

Branded packaging should be geared to the character profile of the target consumer to ensure that it will be positively received. Branding agencies create character profiles of the archetypal target consumer that includes an overview of their likes, motivations, aspirations and other products that they typically use. Having a clear understanding of the target audience will help you to successfully generate a design that consumers respond to well, which will in turn convert into product sales.

| Loyal | Discount | Impulse | Needs-based | Wandering |

The five different types of customers: as posited by sales training consultant, Mark Hunter.

Niki Jones home textiles

Niki Jones collaborated with DB Studio to create the packaging for her high quality home collection (above), that includes linen envelopes and screenprinted potato sacks. 'It was important that the packaging had a similar level of attention to detail as the products,' says Helen Ferguson of DB Studio. The packaging has a clear market sector that it is aiming at – that of high-end interiors – and a clear picture of the type of audience who will buy the products.

< Branding and rebranding   **Audiences and sectors**   Purpose and intent >

Sectors

The market for products is comprised of discrete sectors, such as food and cosmetics, each of which have different needs, demands, sizes and conditions for which different products have accordingly been developed. Within these various market sectors, there are sector cues that a designer needs to become familiar with, which define or suggest where the parameters of audience expectations lie in relation to a particular product category.

These cues are made up of the conventions and shared visual language that have become established about a given product over time, and their presence partly explains why packaging for products within any one sector often look similar. For example, up until a few years ago it was largely unthinkable that a bottle of wine could be sealed in any way other than with a cork. This sector cue was a significant hurdle to overcome during the introduction of screw tops and plastic corks.

The existence and power of sector cues frequently results in shared aesthetics being adopted within the same product categories, which then become a common visual currency for the presentation of competing products within the marketplace. Therefore, innovative packaging design often has to strike a balance between *fitting in* and *standing out* from the generally accepted norms and cues present in a given product sector.

Conventions

Pressure exists for brands to adhere to established conventions, and to stand out only at a micro level; diverging from these norms, or making a bold statement but getting it wrong, can often result in a direct lack of sales. However, a divergent approach can be successful where a product or brand is significantly different or if it manages to precisely capture the zeitgeist of the times.

Product groups often have shared aesthetics, colour palettes and presentation styles. A beer bottle is typically made from green, brown or colourless glass, so consumers expect to see beer bottles in these colours. Likewise, there are things people tend not to expect, such as a washing detergent packaged in a black box. Designers and brand designers should not be restricted by these cues, but should be aware of them in order to have a deeper understanding of consumer behaviour.

Successful products are often instrumental in establishing and adapting cues. These unique characteristics, or 'brand equities', can produce success in terms of brand recognition and sales, so companies seek to protect them from 'me-too' products that try to benefit by copying them. However, there will always be similarities between brands appealing to the same target audience, who respond to the same stimuli; brand equity boundaries will therefore often be crossed.

The paradox of packaging design: the design has to simultaneously fit in *and* stand out.

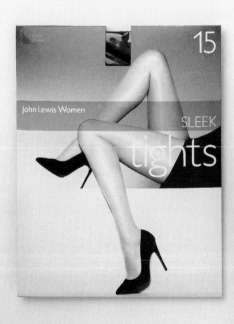

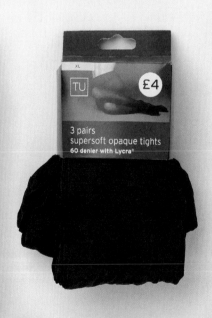

Sector cues

Shown here are three different fast-moving consumer goods (FMCGs) from three different supermarket chains: soap, a packet of coffee and a pair of tights. Each packaging design is unique, but as products in the same market segment, they share certain attributes. The soaps use the colour white to signify purity, and blues and greens to denote cleanliness and freshness. The coffee is all presented in vacuum-sealed packets designed to prevent oxygen oxidising the coffee; this type of packaging has thus become a signifier for freshness. The packaging for tights similarly features images of a model's legs to emphasise the product's sensuality.

< Branding and rebranding   **Audiences and sectors**   Purpose and intent >

Differences between designers and sectors

Designers produce design schemes for a range of diverse products and for companies across many different sectors. Some design agencies dovetail packaging design with general graphic design and thus need to be flexible about embracing a host of ideas, as each sector has its own particular shared visual vocabulary and cues. Other design agencies therefore choose to focus exclusively on packaging design because it requires a specific set of skills that will be different to those required in other sectors of design, such as print design or identity creation. The degree of focus and specialisation required to produce design packaging means that many agencies only choose to offer a bespoke service tailored to meet specific needs.

Packaging design can be perceived as a more ruthless design sector than others, as ultimately it *has* to result in generating sales and making money for the client, which is what they crucially expect to result from the design and is often their main purpose for producing a product. Packaging design has to quite literally deliver the goods, or a product is highly likely to fail.

In general, the retail sector does not have philanthropists paying for products to get to market; companies have to survive by their own efforts and those of their collaborators, such as design agencies. In this context, packaging design forms part of a multidisciplinary approach that corresponds with the marketing and promotional activities of the client.

Within those agencies that only undertake packaging design there are further degrees of specialization, as the mind set and skills needed to work successfully with food packaging are different to what is required for automotive parts packaging, for instance. The ability to specialize is a sign that a design agency has learnt to understand a sector well and that it has a reputation for producing good work rooted in the deeper knowledge it has gained of a chosen sector. The question of whether to specialize or not is one that faces all designers, although in practice the decision may evolve naturally from the type of work that the design agency receives and from the relationships that it has had success in cultivating.

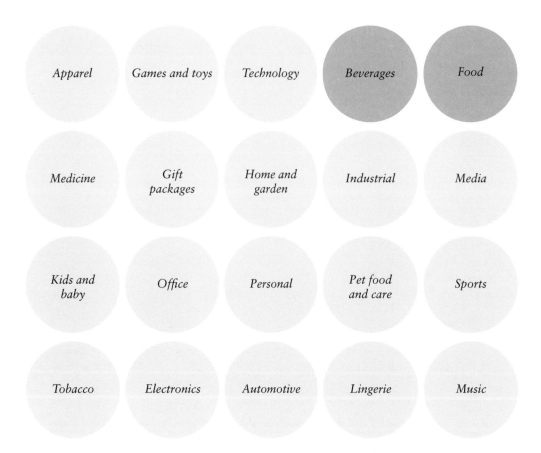

The many different sectors that designers can produce packaging designs for: each have their own specific requirements and considerations. This often leads to sector specialization, or specialization in shared or common sectors, for example in food and beverages (as illustrated by the diagram above), where common knowledge may be transferable.

Australian Homemade

Created by the designer Boy Bastiaens for ice cream and chocolates brand Australian Homemade, this packaging design deliberately steers clear of the typical hi-gloss boxes used for premium chocolate products and instead uses grayboard made from recycled paper – an unusual choice, but one that sits well with the 'profits with principles' business philosophy that sees Aboriginal projects supported with a portion of turnover (right). The packaging is strong, flexible and cheap and has a matt lamination to protect the inside of the box from fat traces when filled with chocolates. The design features a screen-printed logo on the lid and generic product information on the lid's reverse; while various motifs, representing different flavours, are printed with carotene directly onto the chocolates.

Sencida Sport

Flame created the packaging shown (below) for Sencida Sport food supplements, which exemplifies a more direct communicative approach than that in the example above. The design employed here uses the shared common vocabulary that is typical in this market segment, from the large plastic jars, the dark background colour and the abstract molecule symbol to the clear and unequivocal product names. Products in this sector often have a shared visual language.

< Audiences and sectors   **Purpose and intent**   Retail environments >

Purpose and intent
We have so far explored the fact that there are diverse audiences who buy products from different sectors. Within any given sector, the packaging of a brand has two distinct functions: these can be referred to as its *purpose* and its *intent*.

Purpose

Purpose, sometimes called form, concerns what the packaging is physically required to do in order to protect and present a product. Packaging is designed to contain a specific volume or measure of a product, to store it without contamination throughout the transportation process and during its in-store display, to facilitate its easy and efficient handling and stacking, to preserve product qualities for a defined period of time (that is, to ensure that a product remains fresh and does not deteriorate) and to ensure that it is protected against numerous forms of damage, such as moisture, heat, bumps and the impact of being dropped.

Intent

The *intent,* sometimes called the function, of branded packaging is altogether different from its purpose and is concerned with captivating an audience. Within retail environments, a package needs to grab the attention of potential buyers and rapidly communicate various brand values. Its stated ability to successfully satisfy certain needs will lead consumers to view the product favourably and motivate them towards its purchase. Over time, brand communication, combined with repeatedly satisfying consumer needs, can create customer loyalty towards a brand. This can be achieved by constant repetition of the values that buyers are attuned to, thereby fuelling their desire to make repeat purchases.

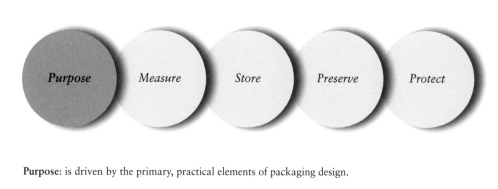

Purpose: is driven by the primary, practical elements of packaging design.

Intent: is driven by the emotional facets that lead us to make a purchase.

Coca-Cola

Each year, Coca-Cola asks a different creative to design artwork for its Club Coke, the aluminum 25cl bottle of Coca-Cola. Fashion designer Karl Lagerfeld created a design for Coca-Cola light (below) that invites consumers to buy into the associated values that the presentation advances; here, those of quality, luxury and exclusivity. The aluminium bottle is much lighter compared to the traditional glass bottle, which reinforces the 'light' quality of the product.

The pop singer Mika created the Happiness Bottle (on the facing page) for Coca-Cola in 2010, which features the use of bold colours inspired by Japanese psychedelic posters from the 1960s. 'I think the few colours that were used are the secret to this bottle, and is why it works. It has this very "design" side to it', asserts Mika.

What do you think of Coke's bespoke bottles and how would you approach packaging such a resiliently universal product?

< Purpose and intent   **Retail environments**   Bespoke to global >

Retail environments

Packaging is often designed for a retail environment, such as in a supermarket, where it will represent one item amongst many thousands displayed on generic shelving. Retail environments can also be created that are sympathetic to packaging needs, such as in a boutique store, where greater control can be exercised over the retail experience.

Generic retail

With around 40,000 different packages to choose from in the average supermarket, across both food and non-food items, the challenge for all products is to stand out from the crowd. Thousands of products compete for shoppers' attention in-store and, according to various research findings, any package on a supermarket shelf has less than three seconds to grab it. Packaging does not necessarily need to be loud or garish, but it must communicate quickly and clearly to the target audience for which it is intended.

The resolve of packaging design for a generic retail space such as a supermarket has a great deal to do with conformity to the pre-established norms and constraints imposed by that environment. Supermarkets are concerned with the ease of handling a product, that its packaging is of a size and durability that will not interfere with its logistics or processes, that it is easy to stack on the shelves and that it will not break. They also tend to use standard-size shelving and lighting, whereby no particular advantage is given to any product other than to its location within that shelving.

The layout design of a supermarket is devised around a well-planned series of encounters designed to entice shoppers to buy. Placing fruit and vegetables near shop entrances creates a positive first impression, while placing staples like milk and bread at the back forces customers to walk past thousands of other lines to get to them. Supermarkets aim to keep people inside and buying.

Impulse purchases

Over 70 per cent of purchase decisions are made at the point of purchase; therefore, obtaining prime locations on shelving is both very competitive and often a privilege that manufacturers are prepared to pay for, in order to display their products where they will be most seen. Such positions include gondola ends and the eye-level shelf. The wider resolve for any individual product is muted or non-existent unless the manufacturer is running an in-store promotion that allows it to use promotional materials, or unless it has acquired a prized gondola end. In this case, the product packaging can be embellished by the use of shelf display material, which draws further attention to both product and brand, such as branded shelf-edging strips and hanging banners that carry a product's livery.

Juxtaposition may also be used to influence buying behaviour. People tend to scan supermarket shelves from left to right, so placing a store brand to the right of a national brand automatically creates an association between products. Likewise, pairing popular items with less popular ones can help to move sales of the latter.

The dual functions of branding and packaging

Branded packaging has a dualistic nature due to the need for its purpose and intent to function in both the pre- and post-purchase environments. Branded product packaging has to stand out and communicate its qualities to consumers more successfully than its competitors. However, for brand loyalty to grow, branded packaging also has to make a successful transition to the consumer's home or wherever the product will be used or kept. The integrity of both the purpose and intent must remain effective once a product has left the retail environment. An outlandish intent may persuade a consumer to buy a product once, but if it looks ridiculous once home, it will reduce the chance of a customer's repeat purchase.

Sanitas

Hatch Design created the packaging for Sanitas skincare products in order to revitalise the brand (facing page). The design is clean and simple and features two squares that unify the product line and have an air of refinement. The use of white space gives the branding room to breathe, so that it can be easily picked out on crowded store shelves.

< Purpose and intent **Retail environments** Bespoke to global >

Boutique retail

A boutique store is a retail environment in which consumers are an essentially captive audience of the manufacturer's brand message, with no environmental competition from other manufacturers' messages present. Such controlled and sympathetic environments allow branded packaging to focus on things other than merely grabbing buyers' attention, as the merchandiser has greater control over the resolve of a brand. The retailer can take and extend the brand characteristics and attributes presented in the packaging design to fill part of or even the entire retail space, if desired.

The resolve can dictate the lighting, the construction materials, the flooring, the size and colouring of the gondolas and the spacing of the shelving; it can also include the insertion of merchandising materials, such as product photos and advertising images.

This level of resolve ties the brand packaging in with any associated advertising campaigns and visual identity in a way that fully immerses the consumer in the product's brand message.

The cosmetics floor of a department store presents a shopper with various different resolves, as each manufacturer typically has a section of a gondola dressed specifically for their products. In a dedicated retail space, the resolve includes the entire area, requiring the creative use of the space available in order to impart the right feel or atmosphere required. This might be achieved using seating and music to create the desired ambience and boutique environment, for instance.

Umberto Giannini

These images show the resolve of a retail space for hair cosmetics brand Umberto Giannini, created by Z3 Design Studio (above and facing page). The calm environment and cool fashion feel means that the products are softly displayed rather than shouting for attention as they would likely do in a supermarket or department store.

< Retail environments   **Bespoke to global**   Solo and range >

Bespoke to global

Packaging and branding has to connect with the particular aspirations and expectations of the target market, and this will vary from one geographic location to another. Designers have to take into account the precise region in which a package will be used and be aware of both the opportunities and limitations that local norms may present.

Appropriateness

There is a great difference between designing packaging for a regional or national market and designing for an international or global market. The communication methods used to reach each of these different markets also necessarily change according to context. For a local product, it may be important to stress the use of locally sourced materials, or that the product meets a particular local need. Humour varies according to region and nation, so its use in a design may not be appropriate for a global product due to the possible lack of translation or transferability.

The messages that packaging transmits need to be pitched at the appropriate level for the anticipated audience. Generally, the more international a product is, the less specific the cultural references need to be. Espousing the virtues of a product designed and made in Britain may have marketing value if it is to be distributed nationally in the UK, but it will have less value at a global level. Exceptions to this rule occur in instances in which a nation is widely recognised for producing certain national products, such as Swiss watches.

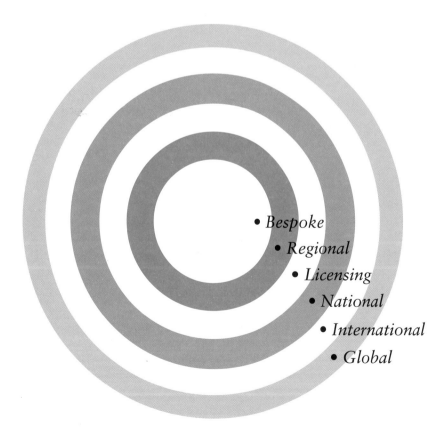

The potential area of influence of a brand: this is represented here by a series of concentric circles (left); from a cottage industry in the centre to the wide reach of a global brand in the outer circles.

• *Bespoke*
• *Regional*
• *Licensing*
• *National*
• *International*
• *Global*

Bespoke

A bespoke industry is one of small-scale production that is typically performed in a home or small premises by the owner and/or their family using their own equipment and resources. Although performed at a small scale, bespoke production can result in very high-quality products. Packaging at this level may focus on the fact that a product is handmade or made with traditional methods, and that it has an artisanal quality due to the use of traditional and/or natural materials. It may stress the uniqueness of each piece or the skilled labour that has gone into its production, the link that the product makes to a forgotten past, and/or the natural materials or ingredients from which it is composed. The physical packaging may use off-the-shelf containers and bags or handmade packaging materials, such as bags and boxes.

Kember & Jones

This packaging was created by DB Studio for Kember & Jones, an upmarket delicatessen and café in Glasgow, Scotland. The owners, Phil Kember and Claire Jones, wanted to adopt a simple, flexible approach to labelling their products. Use of an inexpensive rubber stamp gave a bespoke touch to their labels (below), and reflects the fact that the food is freshly made by hand. A branded circular sticker (above) with a blank space allows the owners to handwrite the labels; they thus look different depending on who made each batch of a given product.

< Retail environments   **Bespoke to global**   Solo and range >

Regional products

Packaging for a regional item may stress cultural traits of the product's origins, or aspects that consumers may associate with the product. Many food products use such regional strategies, particularly when they benefit from 'protected designation of origin' status, such as Cheddar cheese, champagne and certain beers.

In terms of geography, packaging design has to communicate concepts that may initially seem at cross purposes: those of conveying a sense of a particular region that is at the same time able to be interpreted and understood in a much wider sphere than that of the product's indigenous market.

Spaghetti Lunghi N°325

This packaging for Lucio Garofalo Pasta (below), a traditional Italian spaghetti from Napoli, features a mix of wrapping paper and a wraparound label, rather than the cellophane film wrappers that pasta is typically packaged in. It is therefore very noticeable, being nearly twice the length of other brands (as shown). Such uniqueness can be a double-edged sword, however, as the product will only be sold in a niche area of mainstream stores, limiting its exposure to shoppers.

National products

Packaging created for products with national distribution needs to provide a message that is uniformly understood across the whole country. Achieving this broad understanding often means keeping the brand message simple and unequivocal, so that there can be little possibility of misinterpretation or local differentiation. Nationalisation results in a degree of standardisation, a factor that increases with the scale of production and one that is necessary in order to efficiently and cost-effectively undertake wider distribution. This enables the production of standard-size products packaged in the same container no matter where the final destination is.

National brands provide production economies of scale; this means that a product is developed from the same tin can and same paper label regardless of where it will be sold, for example. In this way, products can all be produced on a high scale in one location at a lower unit cost than if different cans or labels were produced in different parts of the country. National brands therefore offer a producer or manufacturer greater economies of scale due to lower unit production costs and they can also benefit from national marketing activities, such as national newspaper and television advertising. For example, a national retailer can use an advertisement for a product in any market instead of having to create several ads with local variations.

moonlight organics

The wine bottles and labels pictured below were designed by Flame for the Moonlight Organics brand, made by the Stellar Organic Winery, and were produced in South Africa. The label design features a hand-drawn image that creates associations with the African provenance of the product, through its depictions of the indigenous landscape and use of vibrant colours, thereby communicating a level of regional information to the consumer about the product's origins.

HARRISON

Steve Harrison is a key figure in British design with an international reputation. Born in Sheffield, he specialised in metalwork and he is particularly famous for his cutlery design. This is a professional collection of mirror with polished stainless steel kitchen knives, well handcrafted in Harrison's mini studio near Sheffield. This collection is carefully handmade with luxury materials. It is one of Harrison's most iconic designs of 2009.

4th

HARRISON

Steve Harrison is a key figure in British design with an international reputation. Born in Sheffield, he specialised in metalwork and he is particularly famous for his cutlery design. Harrison cut down the traditional 11-piece setting to a basic 5-piece set. This set of cutlery is Harrison's most spectacular design which exploits the latest technological advances to arrive at its unique sculptural form.

4th

4th

Kenny J. Huang created this packaging below for kitchenware store 4th in Vancouver, Canada. The packaging tells a story about both the company, which sells products handcrafted by local artists, and the artists themselves. It features earth tone colours to highlight the local craft aspect of the products, along with a signature to identify the creators – such as Masachi Ichuro for the Japanese kitchenware and Steve Harrison for the high end cutlery and kitchen knives shown here.

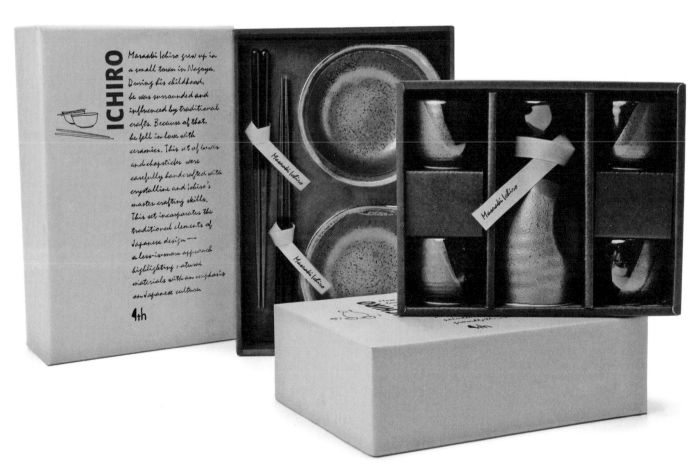

ICHIRO

Masaaki Ichiro grew up in a small town in Nagoya. During his childhood, he was surrounded and influenced by traditional crafts. Because of that, he fell in love with ceramics. This set of bowls and chopsticks were carefully handcrafted with crystalline and Ichiro's master crafting skills. This set incorporates the traditional elements of Japanese design — a less-is-more approach highlighting natural materials with an emphasis on Japanese culture.

4th

< Retail environments   **Bespoke to global**   Solo and range >

International brands

Packaging for international brands seeks to communicate the same message or similar qualities in different international markets. The basic brand concept is likely to be the same or similar in each case, but will perhaps be specifically tailored to the particular requirements and characteristics of each country, in a way that goes beyond merely translating the text from the original packaging or advertising.

An international brand has to use concepts that are recognisable and translatable across different cultures to communicate the brand message successfully, as product usage may differ across countries, as may the contexts within which a product is consumed.

The reputation of the producer may feature more significantly in an international brand and be particularly flagged up in order to project a reassuring brand message to potential consumers that the product is one of quality from a company that exports widely. This can be an effective way to overcome the nuances of product usage in different markets.

Bjørklund

The packaging elements above were created by Sandro Kvernmo of Strømme Throndsen Design for Norwegian kitchen utensils manufacturer, Bjørklund. The branding communicates the high quality attributes of the product to appeal to gastronomes in Norway's national market.

Global brands

Designing packaging for a global brand presents unique challenges because it has to function in a multitude of different countries and cultures. The brand may therefore have to be reduced to communicating one or two key points so that it can be widely transmitted yet remain coherent and instantly recognisable. There is almost no room for geographic differentiation other than through the use of different languages. This presents more of an intellectual challenge to the designer, as it is important to ensure that the design does not offend or fall foul of the cultural norms of distinct national markets. This effectively limits the use of colours, words, images and symbols – in other words, all the elements that a designer has at their disposal.

A simple colour scheme, design and message are frequently used as the hallmarks to achieve global branding, such as the golden arches of fast-food retailer McDonald's, or the green and yellow flower of energy company BP.

Coca-Cola

Coca-Cola, arguably the most famous global brand in history, has developed its branded packaging into one of the most ubiquitous and recognisable pieces of design to be found in virtually every country of the world (above). Coca-Cola has become so linked to the colour red in packaging that it's almost as if the brand has taken ownership of it. The designs shown here were created by Turner Duckworth in collaboration with international advertising agency Wieden + Kennedy.

Royal Horticultural Society

The range of home fragrances above was manufactured by Colony in association with the Royal Horticultural Society in the UK. The range is inspired by the rich variety of UK plant life and features stunning botanical illustrations from the Royal Horticultural Society's Lindley Library, which houses over 20,000 original works. The packaging is simple and understated, so that the focus naturally falls on the wonderful illustrations.

Licensing

On a final note, it is worth considering how licensing works with national, international and even global brands. There is obvious value in a brand being able to align itself with a famous pop star or sports personality. In doing so, they are essentially embodying the *values* of a personality, and applying those to a product and packaging. Licensing is a business arrangement whereby one party contracts to use something from another party for an agreed period of time and for an agreed payment. Licensing is typically used to gain access to a particular product or service, or provides a means to add credibility to a product or service to assist the branding and marketing effort. Product manufacturers may seek to license the use of a particular name or image that resonates well with the target audience or that they hope will cast a favourable light on the product by association. For this reason, sports and music stars are seen as highly desirable for endorsing a wide variety of products.

Brands are licensed or granted by a licensor to licensee organisations that are typically product manufacturers, such as a manufacturer of golf clubs, for instance. In this example, the manufacturer wants to add to the perceived value of its brand to create a higher perceived sense of quality amongst consumers and hopefully achieve higher sales, too.

By signing an endorsement deal with a star golfer, for example, the manufacturer licenses the use of the golf star's name with its products. Before the licensee can manufacture the licensed product, they often work with the licensor in the design of the product as the licensor needs to be sure that the product is of a high enough quality to merit the use of their name and that the association will not diminish their brand value. The golfer often receives a lump sum payment, and perhaps also a royalty, for each use of their name.

The franchise business model is a form of licensing, in that the franchisee buys the right to use a successful product name, marketing materials and products under certain conditions.

Many not-for-profit institutions seek to augment their revenue through sales of products that they do not, or cannot, make themselves. Products are branded with the insignia of the institution and may carry a special detail, such as the illustrations in the example of the Royal Horticultural Society's packaging shown above.

< Bespoke to global   **Solo and range**   Proprietary and own brands >

<u>Solo and range</u>
Packaging designs can be grouped in different ways depending upon the overall sales and marketing strategy that they are part of, as well as to help communicate what it is that they are trying to achieve. Products are typically either individual or solo, or they form part of a wider range. In each case, there are considerations that should be borne in mind.

Solo products
Solo products are those which are conceived of as standalone products and which primarily aim to compete with other standalone products. A box of chocolates, for example, is often branded in a way that means it does not relate to other products from the same manufacturer and will have no direct relationship with the other products made by that company.

The main driver when designing packaging for solo products is relatively simple, in that you are designing something that has to stand out from other products in the segment of the market within which it will be positioned and next to which it will be physically displayed. For example, a box of chocolates may be positioned as a luxury product, but it will be physically placed next to all the other boxes of chocolates in a supermarket. This means that at the moment of making a purchase decision, the buyer will compare this box of chocolates with most of, if not all, the other products that surround it on the shelf. Consequently, the packaging (surface graphics, colour, shape, materials and form) must grab the shopper's attention and rapidly communicate the product benefits to them more successfully than does that of its competitors.

Ranges
Designing packaging for a product range can be quite different to designing for a solo product. A branded product range typically involves a brand being applied to various different, yet similar, products, such as the multiple varieties of biscuits produced by McVitie's. In this instance, the brand instils the same attributes of quality and experience across the range. As McVitie's produces many different types of biscuit, it can present the consumer with a very strong brand statement on one shelf unit via several different products, thereby enabling it to outshout competing brands.

Other brands are used in similar ways across different product ranges like soup, beans and tomato ketchup, such as by the manufacturer Heinz. These products are different but fall within the same general category of food; they also instil the same attributes of quality and experience across the range. However, in this instance, the products may be dispersed around a store by product segment, where they will be forced to compete with other brands in isolation. This means that the branded packaging needs to not only work in conjunction with products of the same brand range, but that it also has to compete strongly *against* other brands.

Retailer own brands, like Marks & Spencer in the UK or Costco in the US, work differently as they are applied to many different ranges of products, from food to hair care. 'Own brands are increasingly taking shelf space from national brands and occupy about 20 per cent of shelf space in retail outlets around the world,' says Kevin Moore, CEO of Crossmark, a North American provider of sales, marketing and merchandising services for manufacturers and retailers in the packaged goods industry. As the retailer ultimately controls the retail space, it can give preference to its own brands and ease pressure from competing brands. In addition, the presence of the own brand throughout the retail environment will continually reinforce it within the mind of the consumer. Own brands may also be varied to reflect different product groups; for example, hair care products or clothing. These are often 'branded' by supermarkets under a different name, as seen in the examples in 'Audiences and sectors' on page 20.

Feitoàmao

Pictured here are various products from different ranges of the Feitoàmao proprietary brand created by Policarpo Design for the Boa Boca Gourmet food store in Portugal. They feature a strong use of colour to identify each flavour, variety and range. These branded product ranges are distinct from that of the retail outlet they were created for and seek to compete strongly against the established brands in the sector.

< Solo and range   **Proprietary and own brands**   Monolithic, endorsed and unique >

Proprietary and own brands
A main distinction that can be made between brands is between *proprietary* brands, and those which are *own brands* – that is, those manufactured by one company to be sold by a retailer, or which are made and sold by the same retailer or outlet.

Proprietary brands
A proprietary brand is a standalone brand that competes with all the other brands in the marketplace. Manufacturers like Persil, Pepsi and Heinz make products that operate in direct competition with other brands. Heinz Baked Beans, for instance, will sit on a shelf alongside other manufacturers' brands and a supermarket's own brand version.

Own brand
Own brands are developed by supermarkets and other retailers, particularly in the areas of food and home products, to offer a broader, more generic appeal to consumers that is firmly tied into the brand of the store itself. Retailers face a real conflict of interest when developing both proprietary and own brands as these will inevitably compete with the established brand

leaders of the market, which are also sold in their shops. Consumers are strongly attracted by established brands, their marketing campaigns and easily recognisable packaging; own brands therefore often seek to cannibalise upon this success.

In the most competitive market segments, retailers and other producers create 'me-too' or 'copycat' brands that closely resemble the attributes of established brands; and through proximity and similarity seek to benefit from and acquire the same consumer favour enjoyed by the brand leaders. Proprietary or own brands increase the number of people that purchase within that segment.

Tesco

Pictured above are cans of soup with brand packaging created by R Design for an own brand line for UK retailer, Tesco. The packaging simply shows a spoonful of each flavour of soup, the spoon an index for the bowl from which the soup will be eaten. The Tesco brand name is reversed out of the label, in an understated way uncommon to mainstream brands.

Look what we found!

Compare this packaging above, created for Look what we found!, a proprietary brand of ready-made soups, with that of Tesco's soups (facing page). The product focuses on the quality of ingredients sourced from local producers (the farmers featured on the packaging) and intends to convey an image of wholesome honesty and authenticity. As a proprietary brand, these soups will have to compete with other standalone brands, and often against own brand alternatives as well.

< Proprietary and own brands   **Monolithic, endorsed and unique**   Luxury and value >

Monolithic, endorsed and unique

Brands can be classified under one of three different general structures, depending upon the extent to which they are original or form part of a larger brand concept, be that *monolithic*, *endorsed* or *unique*. Each structure has its own particular merits and a company will choose one as a function of the overall company structure and brand value, and how effectively (or not) that it can be applied to other products.

Monolithic

A monolithic brand is a single brand used across a range of products to harness the overall prestige, tradition, specialisation and reputation of a company within a market segment; and to make customers aware that it supplies a broad array of products that possess the qualities it is reputed for.

Endorsed

An endorsed brand model has individual brands for different product segments, that are presented as being affiliated to a parent company brand. This approach sees a product benefit from the prestige, tradition and reputation of the parent company, whilst having the freedom to develop segment-specific brands with characteristics to which consumers respond positively. This model is also used by companies that have purchased brands from other companies that they wish to keep alive, yet bring within their own stable of brands.

Unique

The unique brand (sometimes referred to as 'branded') model describes a separate brand that has been developed for each segment without any reference to the parent company brand. This approach gives each brand maximum opportunities for differentiation and specialisation, to thereby appeal to the needs of the market without being encumbered by any perceived negative aspects of the parent brand. However, with no mention of the parent brand, unique brands cannot benefit from its positive characteristics.

The brand structure depends upon the market segments that a company competes in, the strengths and weaknesses of its existing brands and its business model, and the level of competition within the segments that it competes in. A monolithic approach, while lacking a strong parent company brand, is unlikely to add great benefit to different products. A parent brand can help make a new product launch successful, while a launch failure could damage it. Brand structure cannot be easily or quickly changed and so any change must therefore represent a strategic decision taken in accordance with the needs and continued success of the business.

Design considerations

Adopting a monolithic model means that elements of the visual design for a new product will be already predetermined in order for them to conform to the brand. The design for endorsed brands and unique brands, on the other hand, has much greater freedom. For example, premium water company Perrier is owned by Nestlé, but as Nestlé is better known as a chocolate manufacturer, it makes little sense to endorse the water product with this brand, and so Perrier is maintained, positioned and marketed as a separate brand. Perrier also has high-brand equity in its own right that the parent brand is keen to maintain. Yet, if Nestlé were to introduce a new confectionary product, it would make good sense for the brand to be endorsed by Nestlé.

JAQK Cellars

This brand design was created by Hatch for Jaqk Cellars, a new brand of wine that links one pleasure, drinking wine, with another, gaming (facing page). Hatch named the company and each wine, and positioned them under the tagline 'Play a Little'; a novel approach that enabled the wine to stand out in a crowded market. The project included production of a branded e-commerce website that leveraged the design ethics in the form of gift boxes, apparel and playing cards.

< Monolithic, endorsed and unique   **Luxury and value**   Case study >

Luxury and value

Packaging design often associates itself with the qualities of either *luxury* or *value*. Both seek to enhance the appeal of a product to consumers, but by focusing on very different concerns and lifestyles. At a basic level, designing for the luxury market tends to add to the volume of product packaging, while designing for value products often reduces product packaging.

Luxury

Luxury products convey prestige, and this quality is often projected in packaging through the use of high quality or exclusive materials and by presenting a sense of refined aesthetic values. This is perhaps far removed from the generally well-considered design principles of 'form follows function' and 'less is more', but design embraces a wide range of paradoxes. Another design principle stipulates that packaging ought to directly reflect the product; so if the product is high quality and elaborate, it is therefore fitting that its packaging should be too.

Significance

Certain products have significance because they represent certain traits or desires, and therefore acquire a certain meaning. As such, they can become recognised as markers for those traits, desires or meanings. One example of this is Chanel perfume, which is associated with wealth, glamour, style and luxury.

Value

Value, in this context, is a state of mind whereby a person feels that the rewards or benefits that they receive from something are equal to or greater than the effort or expense incurred to obtain it. Value is relative to the individual: a Mercedes Benz car may represent a value purchase to a millionaire, but someone with more modest means will consider it a luxury item. In marketing and branding, value often refers to a low cost option, such as a value pack. Conversely, value can be added through the addition of extra elements.

A brand proposition of luxury or value is presented through the quality of a product's materials and packaging. Creating a luxury product does not always require using high quality or exotic materials, but may result from the crafting of a brand message, supported by branded packaging, that consumers perceive of as high value. The impression of luxury or value can be achieved by branding without intrinsically changing a product. However, product quality does have to be sufficient to support the brand statement.

'The name "eple" was inspired by the first fruit of temptation in the Garden of Eden. The brand represents the company's belief that fruit can be decadent, and that a little indulgence is good for you.'

Wendy Thai, design manager, Ferroconcrete

èple

Ferroconcrete created the packaging design shown here for Pivo Management for the new brand èple, designed for a sophisticated fruit store that is known as the House of Decadent Fruit in Los Angeles, California, USA. Lines are given luxurious touches through the use of ribbons and bows, and transparent packages are used so that consumers can see the glorious colours of the fruit they contain.

Wissotzky Tea (Israel) Ltd
Dan Alexander & Co produced this packaging for Wissotzky Tea (Israel) Ltd, the principal producer and exporter of tea in Israel, to house a range of premium large-leaf teas, infusions and fine blends within delicate pyramid teabags. The packaging features luxurious touches, such as the foil blocking in different colours, which implies the premium quality of the product. The luxury feel is cemented through the combination of the black background and the subtle and understated foil block. The packaging contributes additional functionality to the purchaser's kitchen via the flip-top lid and the brand message is thereby reinforced through consumer use.

'It brings together the legendary tales and magic integrated in the world's tea traditions through icons designed in the spirit of ancient Japanese family symbols.'

Dan Alexander & Co

Waitrose

Lewis Moberly adopted a new approach to generic branding for a basic range of cooking ingredients for Waitrose supermarket in the UK, shown here. The labeling was created for over 60 products sold in generic packages that simply state what the product is, with a light-hearted introduction expressing a suggested measurement for use. The labels create a sense of strong branding due to their consistent and visually arresting typographic presentation. Formality has been replaced by friendly conversation and an ongoing dialogue – giving the user a sense that someone is in the kitchen cooking with them.

< Luxury and value   **Case study**   Student exercise >

Case study
Neäl & Wølf
Propaganda

Within this chapter we have looked at the difference between launching a new brand and redesigning an existing one, both of which come with specific considerations. We also looked at the fact that designs need to fit within sectors and occupy a particular position, be it luxury or basic, proprietary or own brand. Here we take a look at the design of a new brand.

Propaganda were commissioned to launch the Neäl & Wølf start-up brand of hair-care products, a range that was to be sold exclusively in professional salons at a time when consumers were increasingly money conscious due to a looming financial recession. 'With the recession kicking in, women were tightening their belts, and market research told us that women still wanted a premium product but not at the premium price,' says Lee Bennett of Propaganda. The firm's response was to produce Neäl & Wølf products, a range of salon potions that are at once indulgent but affordable.

The brand launch required careful decision-making in order to achieve the goal of producing luxury products on a tight budget. As a start-up brand with a modest budget, they had 'to find a range of off-the-shelf bottles that we could make our own, and that would stand up against the established brands in the field – many of which had bespoke and tooled packaging,' Bennett explains.

'The bottles come in the colours of cherry and pearl that when positioned together in salons are visually striking and impressive. The bottle fronts contain just the logo, descriptor text and a subtle varnished pattern that contrasts against the matt finish of the bottles and gives consumers the "luxury" finish that research told us they desire.'

Propaganda's approach connected with consumers and resulted in a successful brand launch. 'Sales and re-sales so far have exceeded the brand's expectations, and many consumers comment that the first thing they notice about the product is that it is sleek and expensive looking,' Bennett asserts.

Initial design routes

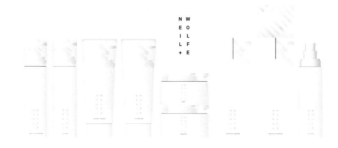

Route 1

Route 2

Route 3

The design development (above) was based around a large, handwritten signature device to convey the idea that the brand had been produced by an influential figure. The first result looked like graffiti and attempts to re-draw it made the logo look too 'street'. 'We ended up hand drawing only the ampersand to act as the signature, and combining it with an upper-case serif font to give us a logo that was elegant and still had the signature effect we were looking for,' explains Bennett.

Design development

The initial bottle designs were all bespoke and used a range of shapes, materials and finishes, as illustrated above, but it was found that this approach was going to prove too expensive and so a range of off-the-shelf bottles had to be found that the designers could brand up. 'Initially the bottles were intended to be high gloss but as we couldn't find a range of all-gloss bottles in the sizes we needed, we opted for a matt range and added a luxurious touch in the form of a subtle gloss pattern,' explains Bennett.

Final design

The final design is simple yet striking, understated and elegant, and shows that high quality, luxurious results can be achieved on a budget by being flexible and optimising the design performance of the material choices available.

< Case study   **Student exercise**   Chapter 2 >

Student exercise
Value

Project set by Nigel Aono-Billson

The packaging design above was created by Ferroconcrete for Pivo
Management for èple, a new brand for a sophisticated fruit store
known as the House of Decadent Fruit (which was originally discussed
on page 45). It challenges us to see fruit in a very different way. The
pack, with its bows and ribbons, embodies a sense of pure pleasure
and indulgence through its emotional message to the consumer of both
luxury and added value. It creates a direct effect and impression on an
individual's perception of fruit.

The staple items we use every day often present
one of the greatest challenges for any designer
to package or repackage. That a package
communicates the brand message is its most
fundamental requirement. It must stand out against
the competition, have an ability to communicate
an emotional message to the consumer and also
impress itself upon on an individual's subconscious.

Packaging was originally created by nature. Just
think of peas in a pod, coconuts, bananas, oranges
or avocados, or of how other fruits and vegetables
are contained or covered in husks, shells, skins,
rinds, chaff or pods. It was humans who then learnt
how to adapt raw materials like burlap or jute
into vessels such as sacks and baskets, and who
discovered how to create clay pots from the earth
for packaging and the transport of items.

A product and its brand identity create its
personality, which becomes the means by which
we identify the product. Here then lies the
designer's challenge when creating a brand identity
for a product and when thinking about how it
will sit amongst its competitors. Colour, shape
and structure play a very important part in the
packaging message. A unique profile, like that of
the Coca-Cola bottle, for example, is unmistakable
and has become a global icon since its creation.

Student exercise:
Adding value to a ubiquitous product

Rice, sugar and coffee are *ubiquitous* products
that we see everywhere. How can a consumer tell
such products apart, or define their value or their
quality? Elaborate packaging places the product
in the high-end sector of the market; does plain
or own-label-looking packaging therefore always
signify or suggest that a product is down-market or
bulk-buy? The product may be straightforward, but
if so, how do you get your brand message across?

You may find that you can create value through
a thoughtful response, in terms of your approach to
and understanding of both the physical attributes
and identity of each product.

1. Create

Choose either rice, sugar or coffee. Using colour, shape and structure, create a distinctly new piece of packaging that clearly communicates its contents. It must stand out against its competitors and precisely convey an emotional message about the product to consumers. Your aim is to produce a unique result, which could become as significant as the Coca-Cola bottle through its uniqueness of shape and branding. You may wish to also consider national and international brand identities, distinct consumer groups, retail outlets and categories that the final product might be placed within; for example, whether it is branded or own label, and whether it will be sold in supermarkets, retail parks, cafés, restaurants, cinemas, theatres or boutiques.

2. Consider:
* shape, form, size and quantities;
* compare with other similar products and brands;
* record all similarities and dissimilarities;
* uniqueness of colours associated with the product;
* uniqueness of packaging structures and materials;
* places the product is displayed.

3. Explore
* Look at all existing identities and brands.
* Compare high quality and low quality.
* Size, shape and construction of containers.
* What materials the packaging is made from.
* How easy is it to see the product inside?

Bibliography and further reading

Chapman, J. N. (2007). *Designers, Visionaries and Other Stories: A Collection of Sustainable Design Essays*. Earthscan Publications Ltd.

Lefteri, C. (2006). *Materials for Inspirational Design*. Rotovision.

Munari, B. (2008). *Design as Art*. Penguin Classics.

Sudjic. D. (2009). *The Language of Things: Design, Luxury, Fashion, Art: how we are seduced by the objects around us*. Penguin.

Thompson, R. (2007). *Manufacturing Processes for Design Professionals*, Thames & Hudson.

Research and concept

The start of any design project involves research to collect information that will be used as the basis for decision-making throughout the design process. The research stage requires the compilation of information about the product, the market, the consumer and the competition, so that the design team has a solid understanding of all the key variables at play as it seeks to find solutions to the design problem.

In general terms, the better that the design problem is understood and the more completely that important characteristics have been identified and isolated, the more likely it is that a successful – and even innovative – solution will be developed. Within this chapter, we will look at how the process works, from devising a meaningful brief through to concept generation and design development.

< Introduction   **Key text**   Responding to briefs >

'Lateral thinking is concerned with the generation of new ideas. There is a curious notion that new ideas have to do with technical invention. This is a very minor aspect of the matter. New ideas are the stuff of change and progress in every field from science to art, from politics to personal happiness.

Lateral thinking is also concerned with breaking out of the concept prisons of old ideas. This leads to changes in attitude and approach; to looking in a different way at things that have always been looked at in the same way. Liberation from old ideas and the stimulation of new ones are twin aspects of lateral thinking.

Lateral thinking is quite distinct from vertical thinking, which is the traditional type of thinking. In vertical thinking, one moves forward by sequential steps, each of which must be justified. The distinction between the two sorts of thinking is sharp. For instance, in lateral thinking one uses information not for its own sake but for its effect. In lateral thinking, one may have to be wrong at some stage in order to achieve a correct solution; in vertical thinking (logic or mathematics) this would be impossible. In lateral thinking, one may deliberately seek out irrelevant information; in vertical thinking one selects only what is relevant.

Lateral thinking is not a substitute for vertical thinking. Both are required. They are complimentary. Lateral thinking is generative. Vertical thinking is selective.'

Edward de Bono, 1970

Key text

Lateral Thinking

Edward de Bono

Edward de Bono's seminal book *Lateral Thinking*, first published in 1970, proposed a new approach to problem solving. This approach can be very helpful when thinking about packaging design. Designers tend to seek patterns in shapes, in colour and in letterforms. If we weren't able to see and remember such patterns, we wouldn't be able to recognise letters of the alphabet, see words and, in turn, read sentences, for example. So patterns can be positives to be exploited.

The negative side of 'pattern-seeking' behaviour, however, is that we tend to rely on things that are familiar. When asked to design a vessel for wine, how many people would create a bottle and remain in the 'prison' of old ideas and the existing way of doing things? When using vertical thinking, we look at bottle designs of the past and build upon them to create a bottle design for the future. This may involve an innovative use of materials or aesthetics, but the object designed would still be a bottle, and its design constrained by vertical thinking.

Using lateral thinking as a design tool, the possibilities are endless. The packaging could take the form of a box, a bag, a package where wine is pre-decanted into glasses, a device that limits the number of glasses served, a pack of concentrated pills to be added to water, or something else entirely. Admittedly, some of these ideas may be impractical and prove too difficult to produce. However, the point is that lateral thinking allows for the generation of alternatives and for an element of chance to enter into the design process, providing designers with the opportunity to escape the 'prison' of old ideas.

This chapter initially looks at how a design team starts a project, from researching the subject matter to the development and understanding of a brief. It could be argued that this approach to thinking can be applied to all stages of a design job, which is not to suggest that lateral thinking is the one and only answer to a design problem. As de Bono says, lateral thinking is rather to be used as a partner to vertical thinking:

'Lateral thinking enhances the effectiveness of vertical thinking. Vertical thinking only develops the ideas generated by lateral thinking. You cannot dig a hole in a different space by digging the same hole deeper. Vertical thinking is used to dig the same hole deeper. Lateral thinking is used to dig a hole in a different place.'

This chapter will raise the following questions:
- Are you willing to accept different ways of thinking?
- What other ways exist to address design problems?
- How can we begin to generate ideas?
- What are the risks involved in trying something new?

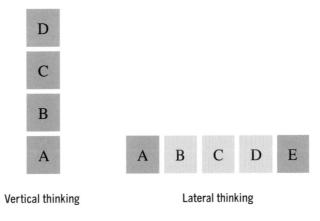

Vertical thinking   Lateral thinking

< Key text   **Responding to briefs**   The design process >

Responding to briefs

The brief for each design job will vary due to the different nature of the product, sector and client involved, and whether it is for a redesign or a new design. However, each brief will have similarities and will contain many standard terms that are routinely used to outline a job.

Agreeing a brief

A brief is a document within which the objectives and requirements for a design job are communicated by the client to the design agency. The brief is often a product of a discussion or negotiation of the intent, the timescales and budget involved, and any other aspects that may have a direct impact on the job.

The more detailed and precise a brief is, the better a design agency will be able to produce a result that meets the requirements and the more likely that the end result will in turn satisfy the client's needs. The process of agreeing a brief requires the design agency to request and obtain information from the client about the job, its aims and the people that the end result will communicate to. This information-gathering process can be summed up in the 'four Ws', as shown below.

The 'four Ws'

The 'four Ws' represents a simple means of requesting the basic information that a design agency needs to have at their disposal in order to be able to begin thinking about how best to approach a design job. Each 'W' represents a key piece of information that will help the designer to determine why a job is being commissioned, what the job is being commissioned for, who the target audience is and where the communication will take place. A designer needs to ask questions to gain information in order to make informed design decisions. If you receive a brief that is *too* brief in nature, it's crucial to request all the extra information that you can. The brief will form the basis of the design process, so if it is vague, the resulting design will be vague. If, however, the brief is thorough, then the design is likely to be equally solid in resolve.

The 'four Ws'

| Who? | What? | Why? | Where? | How? |

Who?

This identifies who the target audience is and includes details such as age range, sex, earning capacity and cultural background. Who is your design being aimed at? Who is the target customer?

What?

This identifies what the product, service or organisation is that will be the subject of the design and communication strategy.

Why?

This identifies the motive or reason why the client feels that it is necessary to embark on a design and communication strategy. Why are they redesigning or creating new packaging? What do they hope it will achieve?

Where?

This identifies the means through which the client would like to deliver the communication that is the result of the design process. Are the client and the designers in agreement about the stages involved in a design process?

How?

How is the design solution that meets the requirements of the brief to be created by the design agency?

New Covent Garden Soup Co

Pictured below is a packaging redesign created by Reach for the UK soup producer, New Covent Garden Soup Co. The design brief set the challenge of updating the brand to position it ahead of its competition in the ready-made chilled soup category, which it had originally successfully created. The success of the product category meant that it had quickly grown from niche to mainstream, which had then attracted fierce competition from major food manufacturers such as Heinz and Baxters, as well as from own label products. To rise above its competition, the brand had to communicate its product story more convincingly than the original packaging (left) whilst retaining its engaging eccentric personality.

Given that the product category was sufficiently established, a soup bowl was no longer needed on the pack, but to compete with the mainstream brands it was important for the company to maintain its quirky personality. This was achieved by presenting images of vegetables on the packaging. Early concepts tested images of beautiful vegetables, but consumer research showed that people generally preferred nobbly ones as they better convey the quirky brand character and are more suggestive of the natural ingredients used in the products. This was presented in the white three-dimensional structure in conjunction with a coloured strip that gave the packaging vital visual equity.

Health and flavour information utilises the top, sloping part of the pack, an area that was previously under-utilised.

The label gives the impression of having been hand-applied.

Idiosyncratic doodles of vegetables and gardening equipment create a feel of care and detail.

The logo is given more prominence in the redesign. It is again applied to look like a logo, while the typography is reminiscent of a shop sign.

The flavour of the soup is given more prominence. This is also rendered, as though it is hand-drawn, reinforcing the handmade theme and style of the packaging.

< Key text   Responding to briefs   The design process >

The briefing process

The briefing process involves the client instructing the design team about the nature of the job to be undertaken, its goals, budget and timescales. The level of detail in a brief can vary considerably, from those where a client is very precise to those that are as vague as 'I need packaging for a new product'. The initial brief is typically worked up by the design team and is then mutually agreed with the client.

The brief will form a document that both parties can refer back to over the course of a design job. During the design process it can be easy to lose sight of the original goals and aims of the project. Referring back to these can help to keep a design direction on track. A brief will often be commissioned, that is to say that the client will work with a third party to develop a meaningful and accurate brief. Once discussed with designers, this brief may be altered, tweaked or even rewritten. The brief will usually contain the following information: what the ambition is; who the packaging is aimed at; where the units will be sold; and who constitutes the target market.

Understanding market position

This refers to a brand's position in the market. A product may be a market leader, a market follower, a 'me- too' product, an own brand or a value product. The market position and aims of the client will inform the development of the brand strategy and the packaging required to achieve this.

Defining objectives

These are the desired results of a branded packaging communication strategy and may be expressed in terms of which target group it will appeal to, the unique selling point (USP) it will present and even a market-share goal that is to be achieved. These will be stated in the design brief and agreed by both the design team and client.

Creating a message

This is the central message that the client desires to communicate through the brand, which will be the driving force and focus of the design. Both the client and design team should clearly understand what the message is. This often focuses on promoting the USP of a brand.

The unique selling point (USP)

This refers to the main advantage or attraction of a product that differentiates it from the competition and that forms the focal point for the design and communication strategy. The USP has to be credible and believable by the target audience and may focus on cost, quality, reputation, service, materials or functionality.

Agreeing key dates and deliverables

Deliverables may include a logo, a brand design, brand livery, packaging creation, a website, display literature and point of sale material to be supplied to deadlines.

Ten rules for commissioning packaging design

Jonathan Sands, of the UK Design Council, advanced ten golden rules for commissioning packaging design, which are outlined below.

1   Conduct a thorough audit of all competitors in your market before you start. Make sure that you understand their respective positioning and attributes, then create your own.

2   Look at what is happening in other markets. For example, if you are just considering the UK or Europe, what is happening in the US or Far East that might give you a point of difference?

3   Put measures in place at the start so that you can track and learn as you go; for example, measure awareness of and attitudes to your packaging now and in the future. A good research agency will tell you how to do this.

4   Choose a design agency based on its track record, not on price, and get testimonials directly from at least three existing clients. Ensure you like them and their work and feel that you can work with them.

5   Be different and ensure that your packaging has its own visual equity, and a strong personality/ attitude.

6   Make sure that your packaging works at all stages of its life cycle, from leaving the factory to ending up in the user's hands.

7   Protect your packaging in terms of trademark law and copyright and make sure that you're not infringing your competitors' rights.

8   Mock up how your packaging would look alongside your competition. Test it in store and make sure that it really does leap out at the point of purchase.

9   Design with tomorrow in mind. Create packaging in keeping with current and future market trends.

10 Do some pre-market testing to make sure that your packaging will find a willing audience. But be careful how you test it, as consumers never quite know what they are looking for until someone shows them something new. Henry Ford once said, 'If I'd listened to what people wanted I'd have built a faster horse!'

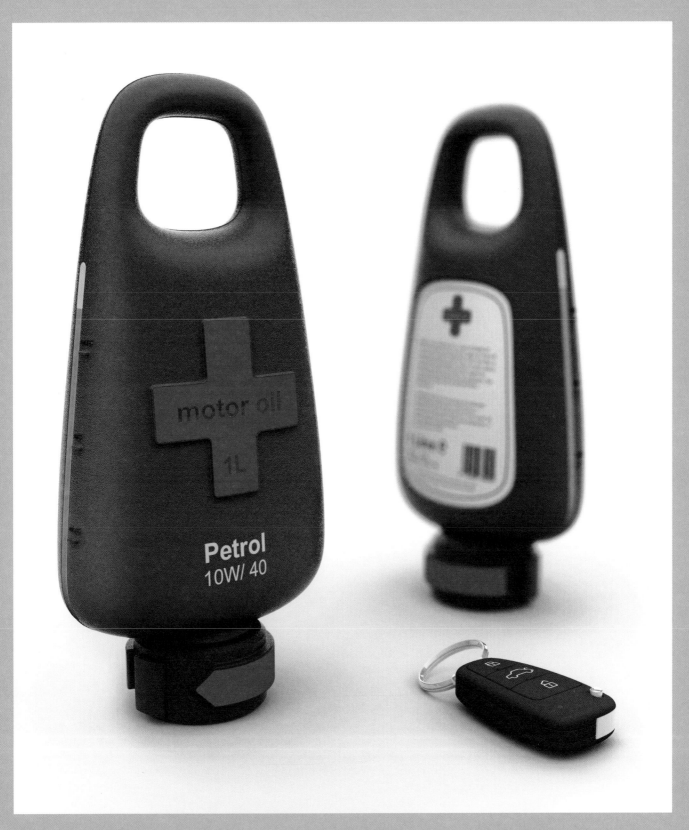

Motor Oil

Pictured is a bottle of motor engine oil that is an example of transformation, as it looks radically different to the bottles typically used for such products. The requirement to present the product in a new way would have been part of the brief. The bottle appears to have been inspired by shower gel bottles as the location of the opening has been moved from the top of the bottle to the bottom to facilitate gravity dispensing, while an aperture at the top acts as a carrying mechanism that makes using the product easier. The bottle follows ergonomic principles as it makes filling an engine with oil less tiring on the hand than stretching it around a heavy bottle.

< Responding to briefs   The design process   Market research >

The design process

Design is a process that turns a brief or requirement into a finished product or design solution. The design process comprises several general stages including: defining the need; researching the problem; generating design concepts and ideas; design idea development and prototyping; design concept selection; design implementation; and feedback to provide a learning mechanism from the process.

Design process steps

Need	*Research*	*Brief*	*Concept and research*	*Development*	*Present*

Identify the need
This initial stage defines why a design project is needed and what the goals are in undertaking it. The more clearly defined the needs and aims of the project are, the simpler it will be to write and agree a brief for the designer to work to.

Initial research
Research aims to acquire a greater understanding of the overall design problem; it is not intended to generate a solution but rather to gather as much useful information about the product, market and target consumer as is possible in order to construct a firm basis upon which to make informed decisions.

Writing a brief
The design team and client need to agree a brief that specifies what the design problem is, what its aims are and what the expected outcome will be, as well as what will be delivered and when. The clearer the brief the better, as both parties will refer back to it throughout the design process.

Brainstorming
The design team will generate ideas and concepts. All ideas can be entertained at this stage from the obvious to the more obscure or extrovert. As the focus is on idea generation, this stage encourages the voicing of all ideas, and various techniques exist to facilitate this.

Early design
The concept generation stage will produce various possible solutions to the design problem. The early design stage sees the best of these further developed and worked up to see how successful they are at solving the design problem.

Selection
A designer will typically present, on average, three design concepts for a client to choose from; one of which will be fully worked up as the design solution. The concepts may be variations upon a common theme or include options that are conservative, adventurous and avant garde in turn.

Basic tenets of the design process

The design process requires a high degree of creativity in a way that is controlled, directed and channelled towards producing a viable, practical solution to the design problem so that it meets or exceeds the stated aims of the design brief. While creativity in design is important, design is an activity that serves economic as well as creative goals. The design process should therefore help to ensure that a design satisfies such considerations by remaining focused on the aims and objectives of the client. The process provides a series of decision stages that will require formal approval by both designer and client, and which will protect both parties in the event of any later disagreements.

At any point of the design process it may be necessary to return to an earlier stage and rework the original design concept; designers should therefore be prepared to review and amend the design scheme if necessary. Not all jobs need to go through all stages of the design process, however; a redesign that uses existing packaging, for example, will not require the same level of prototyping.

Stages of the design process

The design process starts by defining the design problem and the target audience. A clear understanding of the problem and its constraints allows more exact solutions to be generated in order for the project to be successful. The research stage then reviews and/or generates information, including the history of the design problem, end-user research and opinion-led interviews, and identifies potential obstacles. Together, these two stages produce the design brief that instructs a designer and provides the parameters of the design project.

The concept and idea generation stage is where end-user motivations and needs are identified and ideas generated to meet them. The best ideas are developed into a resolve or prototype that can be used for user-group and stakeholder review prior to the design concept being presented to the client. The selection stage involves reviewing the proposed solutions against the design brief and the client then choosing the best idea. The chosen design will be further developed for final delivery, and then produced. Feedback from the client and consumers at the project's end provides a valuable learning tool for designers to gauge their performance by.

Feedback	*Review*	*Development*	*Produce*	*Deliver*	*Access*

People's thoughts	**Review feedback**	**Finding a voice**	**Making it real**	**Prototyping**	**Success?**
People often have a strong initial reaction to a design concept. However, it is important to allow time for ideas to stand for a while. Making the final selection the day after the presentation of the candidate designs allows people to wear an 'idea' to see if it really sticks. It should not be surprising if the preferred option changes after this period of reflection.	Client feedback on the design concepts provides a yardstick with which to assess how well the design team is meeting the criteria of the design brief, how well it answers the design problem set by the brief, and whether there are obvious shortcomings or successes in the design routes that are being advanced.	A design will need to find its own voice and style as it is developed. This might involve the use of photography, illustration and typography, for example, in order to speak to the target audience in a particular way. This vernacular or graphic language is the accent of the design.	Once the design concept is finished, there are still many decisions to be made before it can be produced. Design detailing needs to be considered, such as how the design is going to be produced and printed; for instance, will it require the use of special printing techniques or stocks?	A prototype of the design may be made that can be used for market research with the target market. This feedback may generate suggestions that result in the design being tweaked or radically redesigned. Once definitively agreed, a design will be commercially produced and then delivered to wherever it is to be distributed.	Once a design has been implemented, its success in meeting the aims established in the design brief can be reviewed, and market research can help to identify this. An obvious indicator is whether client product sales have risen or fallen. If a design is not successful, the reasons for this need to be identified so that future efforts can be.

< Responding to briefs   **The design process**   Market research >

Kings

Creative Orchestra designed the packaging shown here for the men's toiletry brand Kings, which was created for sale in the UK retail pharmacy Boots. The newly extended range was created to appeal to users in their late teens and twenties. The designs feature cut-up graphics and typography that give an energy and immediacy to the everyday products.

'People don't want products and services. They want solutions to problems. That's value. And when it comes to solutions, simple is better. Elegant is better still.'

Matthew E May

< The design process   **Market research**   Concept generation >

Market research

The research stage seeks to obtain information that can be used to generate a design that will satisfy the needs of a client. The information generated will be used as the basis of the design decisions that will follow.

The aims of market research

Market research aims to generate a clear idea about the product, its market segment and competitors, the target consumer group, a profile of the target consumer group, and information about the client itself, its history, its brands and so on. All of this information will be fed into the creative process at the idea generation stage. Research can be either quantitative, with hard statistical numbers about the size and composition of target user groups; or qualitative, with information about what that user group buys or consumes and what their lifestyle is like. It may be useful to build up a mental model of a typical user in order to enable the design team to obtain a feel for what would most appeal to them. This could include factors such as education, career, holiday destinations, musical tastes, aspirations and so on.

Primary research

Primary research is the feedback generated during the learning phase of projects previously undertaken; or other information that has been generated first hand, by undertaking surveys, for example. Such information provides a starting point with regards to what worked and what did not work within a specific target group.

Secondary research

Secondary research is information obtained from secondary sources, such as consumer market research reports, industry statistics and other information that may provide a demographic breakdown and historic performance of given markets and market segments. This can provide a clear view of how a market is essentially structured.

Conducting primary research

The results of market research should not be used dogmatically, as all sources can contain errors or biases, may not report the whole story, and can be subject to incorrect interpretations.

Conversely, research can also reveal unpalatable truths. As Paula Scher, of international design agency Pentagram notes, one of the problems with research is that it can be easily dismissed. People also tend to play it safe, in that they generally like what they already know. This means that when you show most people something new and different to what they have experienced before, they will initially be unsure about it; yet they will be generally more receptive when shown something similar to what they have seen before or something that is already familiar.

Shown opposite is a basic guide to how to begin to gather research in the form of a questionnaire.

'In too many instances, I've seen a corporate executive abandon strategy and research because they just didn't like a colour, or a shape, or a material, or a typeface. They just don't like what the thing looks like, or behaves like, regardless of the process and research that helped achieve it.'

Paula Scher, Pentagram, New York

Conducting primary market research

Conducting primary market research can be an effective way of gathering intelligence about the likes and dislikes of the target market. Care needs to be taken when creating a questionnaire so as not to introduce biases or lead the respondents into giving particular answers. Here are some tips on how to do it:

1   The resulting information is only as good as the market research sample. Select a sample group that is representative of your core target population.

2   Design the questionnaire carefully to ensure that it is particularly focused on the information that you need to know, and that the questions do not offend anyone or make them feel uncomfortable.

3   Keep your questionnaire fairly short, as people may not be willing to spend time on completing long forms.

4   Provide some opportunity for detailed answers to be provided so that those people who want to elaborate can do so. Written comments can prove to be some of the most valuable information of all.

5   Determine what your market research recording techniques are. The purpose of market research is to gather and analyse the data, so an appropriate system of recording the data obtained needs to be worked out in advance.

6   Set the criteria for the target consumer beforehand, so that the researcher knows when to stop or redirect the process when it becomes clear that the interviewee may not be a suitable candidate. For research to be meaningful, you will need to determine how many respondents are required for this to be the case.

7   Do not write leading questions, as this will introduce bias into the results by pushing a respondent to answer in a certain way.

8   Use a mixture of open and closed questions. Closed questions are better for finding out quantitative information. For example, the question 'Was the last holiday you took abroad?' is closed, as it can only be responded to with a 'yes' or 'no' answer. Open questions, on the other hand, can obtain more qualitative information; for example, 'Where did you last go on holiday?'.

9   Make sure that the questions make sense. For example, asking 'Was the last holiday you took abroad or within your home country?' as a closed question with a 'yes' or 'no' answer is confusing, as it will not be immediately clear what a respondent will be answering 'yes' or 'no' to.

10 Ask existing customers for their thoughts by providing them with a suggestion card or feedback form.

< The design process   **Market research**   Concept generation >

Koji

Shown on this spread is design development for a new brand of soft drink to be launched in the UK by Reach Design. An important part of the market research involved asking a series of questions to establish the positioning of the brand. These questions, shown opposite, establish a series of key influencers that can be used in the design process. These questions not only place the new brand in a tangible position, but they also act as a reference point to its competitors. It is equally useful and valid to have a clear understanding of what the brand *isn't*, as well as of what the brand *is*. The information gathered here can be used to start initial creative concepts (three routes are shown on the facing page) developed in response to the brief.

The final designs for the three flavours are packaged in bespoke natural glass bottles, aimed at the female health-conscious market. The graphic device on the front is evocative of Eastern notions of balance and conveys a sense of health.

Traditional   Contemporary

What kind of look and feel should it have? The position selected was for calm, fresh, balanced, and old but new, on a scale of traditional versus contemporary.

Novice   Expert

What is likely to be most engaging to our target audience? Naturally elegant and healthy on a scale of novice versus expert.

Fragrance   Pure and natural

Who will be its main competition? Water, flavoured water and diet coke on a scale of fragrance versus pure and natural.

< Market research   **Concept generation**   Ways of thinking >

Concept generation

The concept generation or ideation (idea generation) stage involves starting to generate concepts or ideas that may provide a solution to the problem posed in the design brief. The ideas or concepts will use information obtained during the research stage to direct the creative effort.

A starting point

Designers will draw from several different references as they start to generate design concepts. These can range from a typical consumer profile that may have been developed during the research stage, to a mood board that is a collection of stimuli such as images, phrases, colours and other visual devices that convey a particular mood, to historical and cultural references.

This is the part of the design process where creativity is unleashed as the designer seeks to generate concepts that will subsequently be worked up and resolved during later stages of the process. This stage concerns the potential ideas rather than the vocabulary of the design. The creative effort of the concept generation stage is directed towards the specific end that is established in the design brief, and is informed by the qualitative and quantitative information produced during the research stage. As such, a designer needs to refer back to the brief and the 'four Ws' of who, what, why and where (which were discussed on page 56).

The concept should provide a solution that covers each of these rather than getting bogged down in the detail of graphic tinkering. Ideas need to be tested against the criteria established in the brief to see whether they are relevant and to ensure that they answer all aspects of the problem. Idea generation by its very nature often results from being inspired by something that pops up unexpectedly. This chimerical aspect of the design process is often called the 'creative spark'.

While such spontaneous inspiration undoubtedly plays a role, it is not the overriding aspect, as the design process is typically a formal one within which ideas are often born from progressing through a series of steps or a methodology that has been proven to generate results. Researching a problem, sketching ideas, the use of lateral thinking and the application of different problem-solving techniques can all be used to generate potentially workable solutions to the design brief.

In order to be inspired to produce great work, some designers seek to immerse themselves in the world of the product they are creating for. For example, in order to design packaging for coffee, a designer could visit a coffee house and be a coffee barrister for a day, or visit a coffee roaster or even a coffee plantation in order to get a deeper understanding and better conception of all aspects of the brand and its production. The sounds, smells, feelings and other intangible aspects that surround a product can be as important as the more formal aspects when generating a design solution.

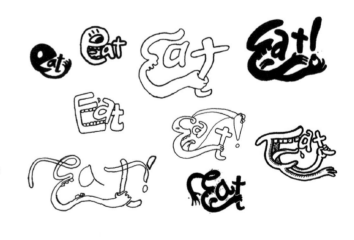

Eat! Ekoaffären

The carrier bags shown above feature an illustration by Axel Hugmark and were created by
Bedow as part of an identity for Eat! Ekoaffären, Sweden's largest organic grocery store. The
illustrations (facing page) show how the Eat! brand name was worked up into the final logo that
was then applied over a wide range of items and applications.

Approaches to innovation

There are many approaches to the subject of innovation, and many academics have attempted to formalise the process. These approaches are non-specific and transferable – meaning that they can be applied to any discipline or activity. Arguably, the most famous example is that of the conglomerate manufacturer Toyota, who place innovation at the very core of its business. In the case of Toyota, the desire to drive innovation is applied to products and literature, as well as to areas as diverse as sewing machine manufacture and car production.

Matthew E Mays produced a manifesto called *The Elegant Solution, Toyota's Formula for Mastering Innovation*, which sets out a number of rules or guides that can be used when mastering innovation. It is claimed that this results in an estimated 3,000 ideas generated every day throughout the company. Its general principles for innovation are outlined below.

1 Let learning lead

'Real learning is a cycle of questioning, experimenting and reflecting. Learning triggers creativity down the line and makes the other nine practices work.' This would require a designer questioning the status quo, looking and thinking about problems in a different way.

2 Learning to see

'Elegant solutions often come from customers – get out more and live in their world.' Immerse yourself in a problem, and all that surrounds it.

3 Design for today

'Make sure you're concentrating on a real need. Don't confuse an unarticulated need with a non-existent one. Don't attempt to manufacture a need. And don't confuse long lead times with future needs.' This is a pitfall to be avoided. Designers often 'stumble' upon a solution, and then construct a need to fit. The solution should follow the need, not the other way around.

4 Think in pictures

'Make your intentions visual – you'll surprise yourself with the image. Start building a visual element into your thinking. Show people the gripping picture of the future by telling the story in a powerful way, using imagery to describe the goal.' A picture paints a thousand words, so aim to capture people's imaginations immediately.

5 Capture the intangible

'The most compelling solutions are often perceptual and emotional. It's the intangibles that differentiate and transform. They move well beyond the transaction, the product, the service, the process. Capture the intangibles that people truly prize and you'll find the most compelling elements of value.' Arguably, this is the hardest of all the stages of innovation to capture. Many brands manage this by having values that transcend the product. Applying a value to a product is a form of narrative. For example, a beer brand may grow to signify relaxation, or the end of a working day; a coffee may be about intimacy or conversation; a food product may represent a lust for life, and so on.

6 Leverage the limits

'All artists work within the confines of their chosen media, and it's the limits that spur creativity. The canvas edge, the marble block, the eight musical notes – the resources are finite. So it's how you view and manage them that makes all the difference.'

7 Master the tension

'Breakthrough thinking demands something to break through. Great innovation is often born of an ability to harmonize opposing tensions. Set goals to conflict with others to prevent compromise and dilution. Breakthrough comes from breaking through the mental barriers erected by the obvious solutions.' This approach would consider the conflicting values which exist in relation to a product; for example, to be the most exclusive and yet the most accessible – this forces the designer to consider routes they may normally dismiss.

8 Run the numbers

'Innovation by definition disrupts the status quo. Digging into relevant data helps fight the dangers of bias, convention and instinct. Great innovations are based on much more than a feeling.' Adding market research, design testing and qualitative and quantitative research can help bolster the case for a design solution.

9 Make Kaizen mandatory

'Pursuing perfection requires great discipline – create a standard, follow it and find a better way. Kaizen ... the concept of continuous improvement, is all about idea submission, not acceptance.' One approach is to make something incrementally better, and when this can't be done anymore, throw in a curve ball by adding additional criteria to make you rethink the product.

10 Keep it lean

'Complexity kills – scale it back, make it simple and let it flow. When it comes to solutions, size and sprawl matter. Be-all, end-all, feature-rich solutions almost always miss the mark because they're over-scoped and too complex.' Continually referring back to the main point of a brief can help to ensure that this is achieved.

Brainstorming

Brainstorming is a creative group approach used to produce ideas for solutions during the concept generation stage. The process is controlled by various steps and rules and seeks to generate many different ideas that will be subsequently pared back to a few workable possibilities for potential development. The brainstorming process starts by defining the problem to be addressed (contained in the brief), selecting group participants who will address it, and forming questions with which to stimulate the creative process.

During the session, participants have free reign to suggest ideas in a non-critical environment in order to discover unusual and potentially useful ideas. Resources such as flip charts or a whiteboard can facilitate the process and allow generated ideas to be noted down. After the session, ideas are classified or grouped by type, where possible, and the practical considerations, implications, benefits, costs and disadvantages of each are assessed to arrive at a shortlist of the best ideas.

A brainstorming session is governed by various rules that aim to create an environment within which creativity can flow uninterruptedly. These include not criticising any ideas, as this prevents people from making suggestions and voicing options. *All* ideas are equally valid in brainstorming.

Work to a target of a certain number of ideas so that people move away from standard thinking in order to achieve it; set a time by which the session should end to keep the pressure on for more ideas to be generated; keep the process manager-free as the presence of line managers may inhibit the flow of ideas; avoid resolve and keep generating ideas during the allotted time as there will be time for resolve later; focus on quantity not quality; and be inclusive so that all group members feel free to openly contribute ideas.

Traidcraft

Pictured (above) is a packaging redesign by Studio Blackburn for recycled tissue products produced by fair trade charity Traidcraft. Without large advertising budgets to show how its fair trade initiatives help fight poverty, product packaging has proved to be an important communication tool; Traidcraft use their products to shout their ethical benefits from the shelf in a friendly, positive way, using speech bubbles and word-play that link product usage with its ethical objectives. The design concept emphasises how each person who buys their products can make a difference by changing the brands they consume.

British Home Stores Chilli Oil

Designed for UK retailer British Home Stores, this packaging by Magnet Harlequin really stands out (left). It is fun and irreverent, with the sombrero bottle top making a distinct point of difference. 'We'd looked at a range of solutions, but as it's primarily a seasonal gift range, we wanted to come up with something that had the initial appeal to drive purchase, yet that was also appreciated by the person on the receiving end,' explains creative director Rik Moran.

< Market research **Concept generation** Ways of thinking >

Design routes

Designers can follow several routes or thought processes to generate ideas. Using different design routes allows a designer to experiment with a range of various ideas and possibilities by viewing the design problem from alternate perspectives. There are two distinct meanings to the term 'design route', both of which will be explored within the context of a packaging design problem.

The first meaning refers to the route or approach that is taken when looking at the problem to hand, of which there are essentially three points of departure: divergence, convergence and transformation, which will be explored further below. It is also possible that the route to be taken will be established as part of the design brief. For example, the brief might be to create a soap packaging that finds a niche in the market (divergence), that fits with similar products (convergence) or that completely breaks the mould (transformation).

Secondly, the term 'design route' also refers to how initial designs are presented to a client or peer group. Presenting just one idea gives no counterpoint to assess it against, which is why initial designs are often presented in a group of three. The designs usually comprise of a series of possible options, including a safe bet (what the client expects), a slightly more adventurous design and something completely off the wall (or radically different from what the client might typically expect).

Divergence

Divergence describes the way in which design thinking spreads out or expands from a central point or theme. Looking at a market to identify new niches that can be targeted by emergent brands or communication strategies is an example of divergence, as is looking for ways to differentiate a product.

Convergence

Convergence moves in the opposite direction to divergence and describes a contraction towards a central, more general point. Generic branding is an example of convergent thinking, where the communication strategy is pared back to something more basic with fewer frills.

Transformation

Transformation involves undergoing a substantial qualitative change. This design route will generate ideas that are consciously different from those used to date and may arise in response to changing market conditions or the availability of new technologies, such as innovative packaging materials. For example, the creation of foil and plastic laminates has allowed marketers to place greater emphasis on freshness and flavour in food products and has thereby signalled a departure from more conventional packaging design presentation.

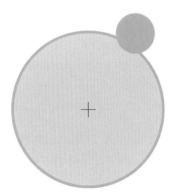 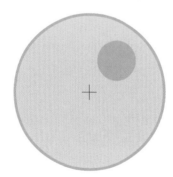 

Divergence: this offers a point of difference and exploits a brand's positioning in order to make it stand out.

Convergence: this involves positioning a brand to ensure that it fits in, is generic, or in order for it to blend seamlessly into its product sector.

Transformation: this requires a brand to break out from the mould and to do something entirely new or present something radically different.

Sterling Nails

Pictured above is a packaging concept created by Little Fury for Sterling Nails for a range of hardware that features durable containers appropriated from other product groups. The nails and nuts are packaged in containers typically used for shoe polish and peanuts to provide a practical storage solution for the home user. The containers provide ample surface space to contain both product information and an illustration.

Uncle Stathis

The packaging below was created by Greek design agency Mouse for the frozen herb range of the Uncle Stathis Brand for General Foods. The innovative, divergent packaging concept is targeted at people that want to 'decorate' their freezers.

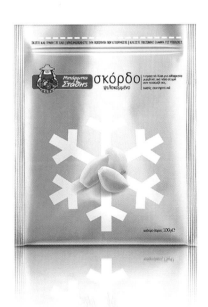

< Concept generation   **Ways of thinking**   The promise >

Ways of thinking
Designers can think about the information involved in a design problem in a range of different ways in order to help them focus on what is most important for generating a solution.

Zigging and zagging
This method involves a designer changing the communication strategy of a brand to move closer to or further away from the strategy employed by the market leader or other competitors to benefit from either using a similar strategy or by differentiating from them. If everyone is zigging, you ought to zag!

Lateral thinking
This is a process of thinking differently from the accepted norms and results in developing novel approaches based on the unique insights gained.

KISS
Keep It Short and Simple, or Keep It Simple, Stupid (KISS) is an acronym that employs the same tenets as Ockham's Razor (see below) and suggests paring back a design to its essential elements. This requires a clear understanding of the message to be communicated and of the audience that it is directed towards.

Focus
A focus on the key message element may allow a design to better communicate to the target market, depending upon how important this element is to them. Examples of this may include the use of terms such as 'value', 'organic' and 'fresh'. Often, a brand will try too hard to be too many things to too many people; focusing on a single element can help to crystallise the design.

Top down and bottom up
This analytical approach looks at a design problem from a system perspective and then 'drills' down to add detail in specific areas (top down); or focuses on basic elements first and works upwards to link these together as part of a system (bottom up).

Ockham's Razor
Ockham's Razor forms the basis of methodological reductionism, whereby unnecessary elements are pared back to produce something simpler, so reducing the risk of inconsistencies or ambiguities.

Python philosophy
Derived from ideas presented by Tim Peters in *The Zen of Python*, these tenets include: beautiful is better than ugly; explicit is better than implicit; simple is better than complex; complex is better than complicated; sparse is better than dense; readability counts; special cases are not special enough to break the rules; practicality beats purity; errors should never pass silently; and refuse the temptation to guess.

White space
The presence of white space allows key design elements to be readily seen, which gives them greater impact. White space doesn't have to be white; it is just neutral space that allows other elements to work properly.

Text minimisation
This tenet suggests that text should be kept to a minimum, with sentences pared back to short, sharp phrases that have a meaningful impact.

Graphic impact
Graphics should create a visual impact that grabs the attention and reinforces text communication, although those that go overboard and are too large, complicated or numerous can be distracting.

User-centred design (UCD)
UCD places the needs, desires and limitations of the user at the centre of every stage of the design process and requires designers to foresee how they are likely to use the resulting product. It is a method that focuses on the goals and tasks associated with the use of a design.

TIMTOWTDI (pronounced 'Tim Toady')
'There is more than one way to do it!'. A problem may have several different, but equally valid, solutions.

'Selfridges Food Hall has long been a destination for food lovers, but it is now less well associated with the brand than with fashion and beauty. This project brings flair to food and communicates Selfridges's core values: being extraordinary, inspiring and captivating.'

Lewis Moberly

Selfridges

The upmarket UK retailer Selfridges commissioned designer Lewis Moberly to create the packaging designs shown here for their food goods. They provide a good example of the application of Ockham's Razor in the minimalist approach taken to the design. Despite the sparse use of text and images, a strong brand identity has been created that avoids uniformity and is humorous.

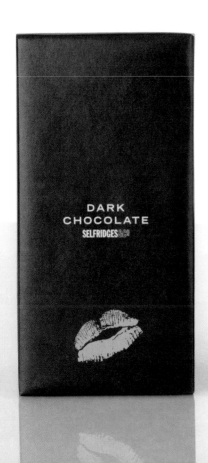

< Concept generation   **Ways of thinking**   The promise >

Selfridges

The design thinking evident within these packaging designs, created for the UK food retailer Selfridges, sits within Lewis Moberley's design scheme shown on the previous page. These designs maintain a specific focus on the prestige of the client through the use of a signature 'S', which was taken from the company's archives and which unifies the range. Presented in a contemporary, eclectic and tactile way, much of the packaging also makes significant use of white or empty space, such as on the champagne bottle pictured below.

CLASSIC
SMOKED SALMON
Along the banks of Loch Fyne, in open box kilns
our salmon is gently smoked over oak chips from old whisky barrels.
Its delicate flavour is evocative of Scotland's oldest traditions,
fishing and distilling.

CHAMPAGNE
PREMIER CRU
ROSÉ

SELFRIDGES

'We may notice, when reaching for a can or a package from a supermarket shelf, that this one looks more attractive than the similar product next to it, but we know little of the skill, judgement and training that have contributed to its special appearance. The fact is that almost every man-made thing around us is "designed", and because we live in a largely man-made environment, designers can be seen as contributing to our quality of life.'

F H K Henrion

< Concept generation   **Ways of thinking**   The promise >

Simplicity

Simplicity is a surprisingly complicated subject and achieving it is not as simple as one might imagine. Design employs many aphorisms, such as 'less is more' and methods such as Ockham's Razor that look to create simplicity in design, on the basis that complexity is not necessary in order to communicate effectively and successfully. Studies by Scott Young and Jonathan Asher at Perception Research Services International (who specialise in consumer research to help marketers connect with shoppers) have demonstrated how simplicity in packaging design can help a brand to stand out among its competitors.

As printing technologies have developed and four-colour printing has become more accessible and cost-effective, there has been a growing tendency for more and more design elements to be added. Retail shelves have become cluttered with bright colours and graphic 'noise' as different brands vie for attention. Yet, eye-tracking studies show that consumers only take in three-to-four elements when initially viewing a package. Simpler designs can thus be more effective at grabbing consumer attention. Less is most definitely more.

Simplicity can involve reducing copy and highlighting only specific product features or values, or making a cleaner design with fewer graphic devices in order to streamline the communication. Creating minimalist designs of white space and sparse typography can also be perceived of as both cheap and generic, however. 'There is danger in taking the call for white space a bit too literally,' assert Young and Asher. Therefore, it is important to balance the use of background space with the strong use of colour and/or dynamic visuals. Creating designs that have simplicity can be achieved by focusing on specific elements, as in the examples outlined below.

Shape
The Perrier bottle's design is reminiscent of a water droplet, and so is suggestive of the product contained within it.

Colour
The yellow of Kodak packaging, the blue of computer giant IBM, or the red tab of Levi's jeans.

Illustration and personification
The Nike swoosh logo represents the wing of the Greek god of victory.

Naming
By creating a unique and individual name, such as Evian water or Elvive haircare.

Brand dynamics

It is arguably much harder to create a design with simplicity for a new, rather than for an existing product, as there is an initial need to convey a lot of information about the brand in order for it to connect with and be accepted by the target consumer group. For example, it must explain the product and its main characteristics in sufficient detail and so that it can be easily heard above the stories of competing brands. As a brand develops, it generates what is called 'brand dynamics' as people's understanding of it grows. Over time, when people see the brand, they will already know something about it, and they may have even used or bought it before.

Coca-Cola provides a prime example of how brand dynamics operate, as it is a product that many people are very familiar with. From this base of knowledge, the messages communicated by packaging design can be pared back and encapsulated instead within the shape of the bottle or red can, for example, with no graphics or information needing to be supplied. Even in this 'naked' state, people would still have an understanding of the brand and would develop a relationship to it. Similarly, the Nike swoosh embodies the brand so effectively that the company does not even need to state its name. Simplicity should always concentrate on the point of difference of a brand, the reason why shoppers should believe in it and what constitutes the point of brand differentiation. Edward de Bono's seminal book *Simplicity* sets out a clear case for the value of simplicity in an increasingly complicated and populated world.

Cultural differences

Cultural differences and preferences are also a factor to consider when considering your design scheme. Minimalism has been popularised by northern Europe (particularly through the modernist movement and typography largely emerging from the Netherlands and Germany); while Asia has traditionally favoured bigger and brighter as better, with simpler packages being associated with basic, low-end products. Similarly, the South American design aesthetic traditionally favours stronger, bolder colours, reflective of those typically used in clothing and decoration. Cultural differences are not static, and in an increasingly globalised and homogenous society, where consumers have ever more experience of other cultures, these particularities of culture become increasingly less distinct. Using simplicity well requires that the packaging is not perceived as boring, dull or uninformative, and that the design is brave and clear in expressing the brand's single most powerful aspect.

P&P

Pictured is a design created by Creasence for a 12-inch vinyl record
by DJ Pinch and Pavel Ambiont for the Pinch and Pavel label. The
packaging makes explicit use of the three basic shapes explored
by the Bauhaus, which are shapes adopted by the music and video
reproduction equipment industry to represent the stop, play, forward
and rewind of tape flow. The triangle and square are printed onto the
label while the circle appears more subtly and is formed from the die-
cut in the sleeve.

< Concept generation   **Ways of thinking**   The promise >

*'Simplicity before
understanding is simplistic;
simplicity after understanding
is simple.'*

Edward De Bono

Τα αόρατα ρούχα του βασιλιά
Hans Christian Andersen

Πριν από πολλά...
... πολλά χρόνια, ζούσε ένας βασιλιάς που του άρεσαν τα όμορφα
ρούχα. Μια μέρα, δύο κατεργάρηδες κατέφτασαν στην πόλη του.
Είπαν πως είναι υφαντές και πως ήξεραν να υφαίνουν πανέμορφα
κι αραχνοΰφαντα ρούχα, από ένα μαγικό πανί που μονάχα οι
ανίκανοι και οι ανόητοι δεν μπορούσαν να το δουν. «Σπουδαία ιδέα»,
σκέφτηκε ο βασιλιάς. «Έτσι θα μάθω ποιοι από τους ανθρώπους
μου είναι ανίκανοι και θα μπορώ να ξεχωρίζω τους έξυπνους από
τους βλάκες». Κι έδωσε αμέσως στους δύο κατεργάρηδες ένα
πουγκί γεμάτο χρυσά για να αρχίσουν να υφαίνουν το πανί τους.
Αμέσως εκείνοι καμώθηκαν πως έπιασαν δουλειά μπροστά στους
αδειανούς αργαλειούς τους.
Οι μέρες περνούσαν. «Θα στείλω τον καλύτερό μου υπουργό να δει
τι κάνουν», σκέφτηκε ο βασιλιάς. Έτσι κι έγινε. «Θεέ μου!» σκέφτηκε
ο γερο-υπουργός μόλις βρέθηκε μπροστά στους αργαλειούς.
«Δεν βλέπω τίποτα!» Μα δεν το είπε φωναχτά. Οι δύο κατεργάρηδες
του έδειχναν δεξιά κι αριστερά, μα εκείνος πάλι δεν έβλεπε τίποτα.
«Αχ, γιατί;» έλεγε μέσα του. «Να είμαι άραγε τόσο ανίκανος, τόσο
βλάκας;». «Δεν λες τίποτα;» του πέταξε ο ένας από τους δύο.
«Ω, μα είναι υπέροχα, τα καλύτερα!» είπε ο γερο-υπουργός.
«Τι σχέδια! Και τι χρώματα! Τρέχω αμέσως να το πω στον βασιλιά!»
Κι έτσι οι δύο κατεργάρηδες τσέπωσαν κι άλλα χρυσά κι εξακολού-
θησαν να υφαίνουν μπροστά στους αδειανούς αργαλειούς τους.
Ο βασιλιάς ξανάστειλε πολλές φορές να δει την πρόοδό τους.
«Εξαίσια!» του έλεγαν όλοι, ρούχα αντάξια για να τα φορέσει στη
μεγάλη παρέλαση. Ο βασιλιάς γέμισε τους δύο κατεργάρηδες με
πολλά παράσημα.

Την παραμονή...
... της παρέλασης ξενύχτησαν για να αποτελειώσουν τα ρούχα.
Καμώνονταν πως έκοβαν το πανί στον αέρα με μεγάλα ψαλίδια
και πως έραβαν με βελόνες χωρίς κλωστή. «Έτοιμα!», ανακοίνωσαν
με μια φωνή.
Ο βασιλιάς γδύθηκε και οι δύο κατεργάρηδες καμώθηκαν πως
τον έντυναν με τα καινούργια ρούχα. Ανήμερα της παρέλασης,
ο βασιλιάς βγήκε με τα καινούργια ρούχα από το παλάτι του στους
δρόμους. Κρεμασμένοι σαν τσαμπιά από τα παράθυρα, οι υπήκοοι
του φώναζαν: «Δέστε πόσο του πάνε τα καινούργια ρούχα του
βασιλιά μας!». Κανείς τους δεν ήθελε να παραδεχτεί πως δεν έβλεπε
τίποτα, επειδή τότε θα ήταν σαν να έλεγε πως ο βασιλιάς τους ήταν
ανίκανος και βλάκας.
«Μα αυτός δεν φοράει τίποτα!», φώναξε ξαφνικά ένα παιδάκι.
«Ένα παιδάκι λέει πως ο βασιλιάς είναι γυμνός!», είπε ένας άλλος.
Και ύστερα κι άλλος, κι άλλος, κι άλλοι πολλοί μαζί:

«Ο βασιλιάς είναι γυμνός!».

Ο βασιλιάς...
... ένιωσε να τον πιάνει σύγκρυο. Ήξερε πως έλεγαν την αλήθεια,
μα εξακολούθησε να βαδίζει επικεφαλής της πομπής, ενώ πίσω του
οι βαλέδες του κρατούσαν ψηλά τον ποδόγυρο από την ανύπαρκτη
φορεσιά του για να μη σέρνεται στο χώμα.

Naked King

Shown on this spread is the visual identity and brand packaging
created by Beetroot, Greece, for a new winemaker and a new wine.
The high-quality wine is free from chemical treatment and so is natural
and organic. The client referred to it being a 'king of wines', which
reminded the design team of the Hans Christian Andersen story, *The
Emperor's New Clothes*, in which the king sits naked for everyone to
see. This led to the wine being called Naked King, which was visually
presented by a crown-shaped, die-cut and embossed label. 'We wanted
it to seem like a naked king, without anything on,' explains Beetroot.
The wooden presentation box was screen-printed with the story set
in large type, like a children's book. The design team resisted the
temptation to add additional elements in order to keep the design
simple and unadorned, and so present a true reflection of the natural
product contained within it.

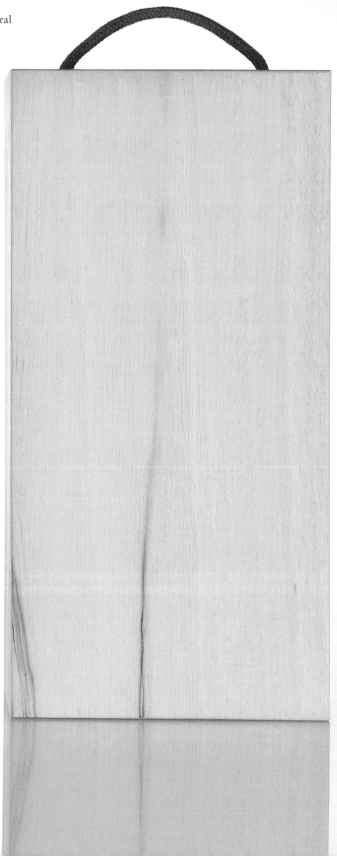

< Ways of thinking   **The promise**   Rethinking the expected (transformation) >

The promise

Packaging communicates a *promise*: a commitment from a seller to a buyer about the benefits of a product. A buyer can either accept this promise or not. This interaction of values is performed at the moment a consumer glances at a product on a shelf and forms an opinion about what the product is and its potential benefits and negative aspects.

The need for honesty

The ability to communicate so much information in a single design brings with it the responsibility to be honest regarding the claims made about a product. The promise that a product makes to a consumer needs to be a fair representation of the combination of product values and attributes, so that a consumer's expectations can be fulfilled through product use. There is little value in deceiving a consumer, as they will not repeat purchase and will switch to a competing brand that better lives up to its promises.

While brand communications often talk up or even exaggerate product attributes, they must not make the product out to be something that it is not. The need to be honest does not mean that product packaging cannot be creative and exciting however; rather, it simply means that packaging should not promise something that the product cannot deliver.

Fulfilling the promise

If constructed well, the promise essentially creates a closed loop that stimulates repeat purchases. If, however, the product doesn't live up to the promise made, then the loop will be broken. Equally, a good product won't survive if the packaging simply hasn't been good enough to create sufficient initial sales.

The various elements explored in this chapter, such as approaches to innovation, ways of thinking and design directions, can be used to distil the essence of a brand into something tangible, whether this is a value, an attribute, an ambition, a desire or a benefit of the product that can be communicated to the target audience. These distilled product 'promises' can be articulated through design direction and graphic narratives, and through the use of imagery, typefaces, colour and the shape and form of a given design.

The promise of a product: this is constructed by establishing its values, attributes, ambitions, desires and benefits.

REALLY REFRESHING TONIC

Tonic
Voor de jonge onzuivere huid
Anti-bacterieel, bestandsdeel,
hamamelis

Tonique
Peaux jeunes à problèmes agent
Antibactérien hamamelis

Stärkungsmittel
Für junge unreine Haut
Antibacterien, hamamelis

I WILL SAVE YOU FROM SPOTS

Tonic depper
Voor de jonge onzuivere huid
Met zinc PCA en hamamelis

Tonique stick
Pour les peaux jeunes à impuretés
Au zinc PCA et hamamelis

Stärkungsmittel stick
Für die junge unreite Haut
Mit Zink PCA und Hamamelis

YOUR FACE WILL BE SUPER SQUEEKY CLEAN

YOUR FACE NEEDS ME TOO!

HEMA Skincare

Pictured above is the packaging created by Studio Kluif for skincare products for European retailer Hema, which features surface graphics that tell the consumer exactly what the products will do for them. This unambiguous, no-nonsense approach establishes an honesty with the consumer and immediately reflects the product benefits.

Criterio

Lavernia & Cienfuegos created the packaging below for RNB laboratories for its Criterio fragrance for men. It features a transparent glass polyhedron with edges and planes that create a double sensation; of hardness on one side and luxury on the other, which together combine to suggest a sense of masculine elegance.

< The promise   **Rethinking the expected (transformation)**   Case study >

Rethinking the expected (transformation)

Innovation involves a change in the way that something is performed or designed in order to improve it in some way. Innovation often involves doing something substantially different and rethinking something that already exists. Packaging provides many examples of innovation; of the seemingly constant process of rethinking to make improvements that may make a product easier to use, or which may extend its shelf life, better protect it, facilitate its distribution and increase its consumer appeal.

The need for invention
What is the need for invention? Why does packaging have to continually change? Two clear motivations behind this drive for innovation might be identified: to meet and maintain the minimum requirements expected by the market; and to make a breakthrough that enables a producer to more readily differentiate their product in the marketplace. In most cases, this second factor (a well-defined brand identity) quickly creates the former (being a strong market competitor); for example, food packaging constantly evolves and uses new materials to ensure that the contents are ever fresher and crisper. Any successful innovation will quickly become copied by a company's competitors, as each invention sets a new benchmark of what buyers have come to expect.

Innovation as a means to problem-solve
Invention can be usefully directed to solve practical problems. As people become increasingly concerned about the environmental impacts of what they do, buy and consume, packaging options are being re-addressed with the environmental design mantra of 'reduce, reuse and recycle' in mind. This design ethos has come to be applied through, for instance, reducing the thickness of bottles and cans so that they consume less material, creating packaging that can have a subsequent use, and making packaging easier to recycle by reducing the number of different materials that it contains.

Designers also seek to innovate in order to find new ways to solve problems and to present different solutions to those currently in use. Successful invention and innovation requires a thorough understanding of the product or problem at hand. It also demands the ability to think through all aspects of packaging, delivery and consumption, from which may arise possible alternative solutions to current practices, the use of materials and so on. Such attention to detail can help to uncover or determine any potentially fundamental flaws that may be implicit within existing solutions, as well as to identify what it is that producers or consumers really want.

Inventiveness can also often involve injecting an element of fun into a product, such as with the novel mayonnaise caps shown on the facing page, which offer a slightly different delivery method of a familiar, everyday product. Making small changes such as this can ultimately have a big impact.

Kavli

Strømme Throndsen Design created this innovative lid (shown below) for the launch of Kavli mayonnaise in Norway. The patented adjustable lid allows the user to choose whether the mayonnaise comes out of the tube in a thick, thin or shoestring flow. This provides an interesting example of incremental innovation; the design team took something that already existed and changed it, so making it both look and function differently and to great effect.

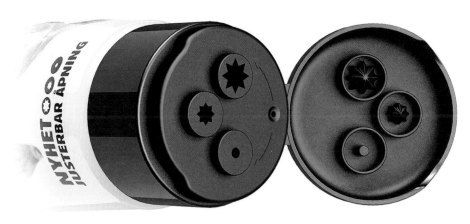

< The promise   **Rethinking the expected (transformation)**   Case study >

'*Can you imagine going through even a single day without interacting with numerous objects that are packaged? Unlikely! In today's environment, virtually everything is packaged.*'

The Visionary Package – Herbert Meyers and Richard Gerstman

1 Litre Water™

Water is a product that is essentially a commodity, so it can prove difficult to differentiate it from its market competitors. Producers might choose to add carbon dioxide gas or artificial or natural flavours to it, but at the end of the day the product is still water. How can something distinctive and eye-catching be created to ensure that consumers will purchase it?

The main way in which bottled water is branded and differentiated is through its packaging. The water bottle shown here was created for the 1 Litre Water™ company and features an integrated drinking cup as part of its award-winning design. The resulting package is highly functional, sophisticated, elegant and visually appealing. A spokesperson for 1 Litre Water™ says: 'Our proprietary design has been acknowledged as the most functional, sophisticated and visually appealing bottle on the market.' Its clean lines exude exclusivity and refinement, and the integrated cup distinguishes the product as one likely to be chosen by the more discerning customer who does not want to be seen swigging directly from a water bottle.

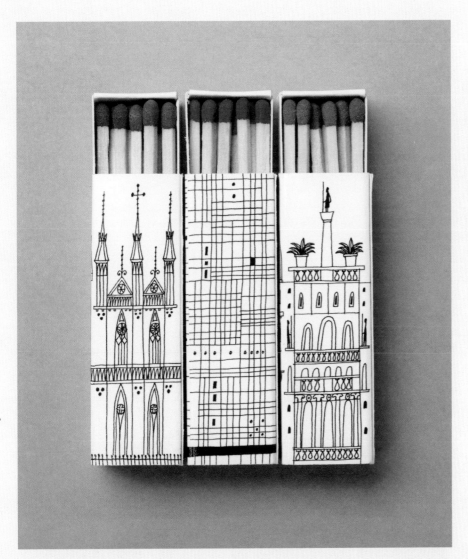

Arkitekturmuseet

These unique matchboxes cleverly present a rethink of the expected and were created by Happy Forsman & Bodenfors for Arkitekturmuseet, the Swedish Museum of Architecture, and feature illustrations by Klas Fahlén. Instead of a matchbox, we are rather confronted by different blocks that form part of a matchbox city comprising different architectural styles, including the Renaissance, Gothic and International, that are intended to inspire people to learn more about architecture.

< Rethinking the expected (transformation)   **Case study**   Student exercise >

Case study
Longview vineyard
Voice

After Australian vineyard Longview was sold, the new owners commissioned a label redesign with the aim of portraying a message of quality and uniqueness, and increasing sales among the 25–45 year olds target group within the A$20–45 price range. Pictured on this and the following spread are designs created by Voice for Longview.

Longview produced a short run of seventy magnums of its Devil's Elbow Cabernet Sauvignon and Yakka Shiraz as promotional gifts for business clients, shown here. Black-and-white illustrations were created by Voice to resemble the diverse names of the wines with a related graphic image in an engraving style, to give them a common voice and appearance while remaining clear, distinctive and sharp. The typography, stock and illustration style are all characteristic of the hands-on, contemporary nature of the vineyard.

As well as creating new bottle labels, Voice commissioned the production of custom-designed cardboard cylinders to house the magnums, each of which wears the reworked original label artwork, and expands on the stories behind each wine. The cylinder for Devil's Elbow features road signage and so relates to a notorious corner on the road to the vineyard; Yakka is named after peculiar plants that scatter the vineyard – its cylinder is adorned with 19th century botanical illustrations.

< Rethinking the expected (transformation)   **Case study**   Student exercise >

When Voice was given the task of designing the packaging for Longview Vineyard's sparkling wine, W.Wagtail, it recognised the importance of creating something that really stood out. Drawing on the personality of the wine's namesake, Willy Wagtail, Voice created a label on the styling of a bird watchers' membership certificate (top left) from the 1940s.

The ornithological subject matter was an opportunity to feature local birdlife and the flora that exists around the vineyard, hinting at the fruity and colourful flavours of the wine. Voice re-drew the entire certificate from scratch and created the fictitious Longview Sparkling Wine Society in order to maintain the soul and structure of the original vintage certificate and its list of patrons and committee members.

Voice used an image of Saturn for the Nebbiolo Riserva (far left), the Roman god of agriculture and harvest, as the family name behind the product is Saturno. A scraperboard illustration was screen-printed directly onto the bottle to ensure that the visual aesthetic maintained a sense of Roman mythology.

The objective for the Longview Epitome Late Harvest Riesling (left) was to create a unique label aimed at a target audience of females aged 25 and up. The label (above) takes its form from a doily, and is a reference to the type of food that is typically consumed with sweet dessert wine. The delicate pattern of the doily creates a sense of elegance and quality that appeals to its target audience and visually sets the wine apart from its competition.

< Case study   Student exercise   Chapter 3 >

Student exercise

Reinvention

Project set by Nigel Aono-Billson

Revisited above is a packaging design that has succeeded in reinventing its market sector through packaging alone, rather than through an overall reinvention of the product itself (this project was originally discussed on page 86). The 1 Litre Water™ company bottle creates a point of difference to distinguish its given brand identity through the use of innovative packaging – a point of difference that would be hard to make through the product alone.

Designers are often asked to completely rethink the packaging approach adopted for a specific product or class of products, such as by taking an everyday product or item and cleverly re-appropriating it. The product will still remain the same but the change taken to the packaging approach can radically alter consumer perception of it.

As we saw at the beginning of this chapter, the design problem can be approached through the use of lateral thinking processes. Employing what de Bono terms 'vertical' and 'lateral' thinking, it is possible to devise different design approaches which far exceed the normal or expected solution.

Take a regular domestic item that you might find on any shelf in a cupboard or even in the fridge. Consider how this item could be successfully repackaged to make it at least one of the following:

- more functional and/or effective;
- ethical;
- socially responsible.

By simply considering how you could improve a product or series of products using lateral thinking, you can envisage and bring about a new series of approaches to the design problems likely to be encountered during the process of redesign, as well as considering ways in which these changes might be effectively implemented.

Student exercise

How to package an egg

Quite often, when we buy eggs in reformed paper carton containers, we find upon opening the box that one, two or even more of the eggs are either cracked or smashed.

The egg is a fragile item that can be easily broken if not treated or handled correctly. By using lateral thinking, consider how you might create a new means of protection for transporting and packaging eggs, in the form of an outer shell or casing, or package of some description.

This could take the form of a wrap or protective boundary that would not only allow the user to carry the eggs, but which would also be convenient for their storage as well. This casing should be created in a form or format that is unlike any container or package that currently exists or that has formerly been deployed for this purpose.

Try to give the product a point of difference through the packaging alone; it is hard to do this through the product itself given that it is difficult to distinguish one egg from another (in terms of their form, if not entirely in terms of their 'promise').

1. Create

A new structure, form, carrier and protector that is both strong but light, and using a minimum of materials. This could contain one or more eggs, could double as storage and might also form part of a system. It has to be: recyclable, environmentally friendly and easy to dispose of, too. If the container were to be dropped or knocked, for example, the packaging would need to ensure that the egg/s would not be broken or damaged. You may also wish to consider how it might be recognised and sold according to its purpose.

2. Consider:

- its form, size and structure;
- how it compares with similar items of its kind;
- all of its similarities and dissimilarities;
- its unique qualities;
- its shelf life and usable time limits.

3. Explore:

- existing forms of packaging in this market;
- the size, shape and construction of current product containers;
- what materials existing forms of packaging are made from;
- how easy it is to break an egg;
- how easy it is to crush or destroy the packaging.

Bibliography and further reading

Kirkpatrick, J. (2009). *New Packaging Design*. Laurence King Publishing.

Klanten, R. Ehmann, S. (2009). *Boxed and Labelled: New Approaches to Packaging Design*. Die Gestalten Verlag.

Pepin Press, (2003). *Structural Package Designs (Packaging and Folding)*. Agile Rabbit.

Williams, N. (2005). *More Paperwork: Exploring the Potential of Paper in Design and Architecture*. Phaidon Press.

Design approaches

Designers often take different approaches when creating branded packaging for a product in order to highlight its qualities, characteristics and attributes. These diverse approaches comprise a toolkit that can be used to generate solutions to solve design problems in a range of ways. This chapter will introduce these various different approaches and show how they can be used to generate design solutions. Each approach focuses on certain key aspects of the product that are important in the purchase decision.

These may be used to persuade a consumer about the product's quality, to establish a point of difference from the competition, to stress the history and experience of the manufacturer or to emphasise aspects of the brand itself. Humour is also frequently used to establish direct communication with a particular target consumer group.

< Introduction   Key text   Visual shorthand >

'In the cities in which we live, all of us see hundreds of publicity images every day of our lives. No other kind of image confronts us so frequently.

In no other form of society in history has there been such a concentration of images, such a density of visual messages.

One may remember or forget these messages but briefly one takes them in, and for that moment they stimulate the imagination by way of either memory or expectation. The publicity image belongs to the moment. We see it as we turn a page, as we turn a corner, as a vehicle passes us. Or we see it on a television screen whilst waiting for the commercial break to end. Publicity images also belong to the moment in the sense that they must be continually renewed and made up-to-date. Yet they never speak of the present. Often they refer to the past and always they speak of the future.'

John Berger, 1972

Packaging design contains various diverse elements that work together to meet the design objectives, such as type, images, lettering, icons and other graphics, as well as the use of space. Individual designers will select and use these elements in particular unique ways. Specific elements are chosen by designers because of the impact they will have on the packaging design, their ability to convey the qualities of the brand, and because of their effectiveness at grabbing our attention, that quality which makes us 'briefly take them in' as Berger puts it in the introductory essay to *Ways of Seeing*.

Each design approach seeks to make the elements of a design communicate above and beyond what it is. How the elements are presented and how the inter-relationships between them create channels of communication affect how we then receive and interpret that information. Semiotics explains how graphics communicate as signs and symbols, and demonstrates how cognitive meanings are based on the knowledge that we acquire through perception, intuition and reasoning, while denotive meanings directly refer to something. Food packaging often features an image of the food on its front, which represents a denotive communication of what the package contains, for example.

As Berger suggests, the volume of branded messages we receive each day from packaging means that we have become highly sophisticated in interpreting and understanding such communications to the extent that marketers have a good idea of which communication strategies and design approaches work best for distinct product types or consumer groups. These are the sector cues and brand equity that we explored in chapter 1. The strongly targeted nature of such communications means that they can readily exert a powerful influence on our lives and behaviour.

This chapter will look at colour, branding, personality, humour, persuasion, materials, attributes and experience, which each offer a different approach to solving a design problem. The seemingly simple choice of colouring something blue, for instance, involves making a creative decision, because variant hues and tones of blue have especial symbolic references and cognitive meanings. Is the hue a royal blue, reflex blue or sky blue? Does it have a classic or modern feel? Each approach implies dealing with sometimes strong cultural meanings that can be used to help build a narrative for a design.

If a brand were to be represented by an image of a woman, what type of woman would she be? Would she be old or young? How would she be dressed? What ethnic background would she be from? Would she wear make-up? Each decision would need to be made, refined and checked throughout the design process to ensure that it stayed true to the aims of the brand, as design elements may also carry some meanings and interpretations that you do not especially want them to.

Two women are pictured below to illustrate the distinctive results that distant approaches to design can achieve. On the left is a contemporary colour photograph and on the right is a Renaissance-era portrait by Antonio del Pollaiolo (c.1432–1498). Both women are shown in profile and both show exposed skin on the shoulders and neck; one has a more formal, rigid pose while the other is more spontaneous and joyful. Yet, they obviously belong to two very different historical periods characterised by very contradistinct moralities, hopes and expectations.

This example, like this chapter, raises the following questions:
- How can different approaches be used to create a powerful communication narrative?
- Why is it important for design elements to make a visual impact?

< Key text   **Visual shorthand**   Branding, language and colour >

Visual shorthand

Visual shorthand works by representing a product on the packaging with a sign. This can also be referred to as the signifier and the signified. The signifier is a sign, a representation or drawing, while the signified is the product. Designers frequently look for ways to distil an idea or concept into a graphic device that is simple and clear to understand, and the use of symbols and graphics aids this process.

The signifier and the signified

Creating a signifier or representation of something is a method that can be used for most products and is something that can readily be incorporated into the visual aspects of packaging design. The trick is in identifying, or distilling, the essential element within the product that can be easily recognised and projected by a simple reference or sign.

Common visual currency

Symbols can be used to signify a product or concept and these can be abstract or realistic. Symbols work as a visual device because the viewing audience interprets them in a certain way due to the shared cultural and social norms that they tap into. As such, this body of symbols can be referred to as a common visual currency; that is, a set of general references that are commonly understood by the broader population at large. In our daily lives, we are surrounded by symbols that we subconsciously interpret and understand with instant impact. A cross, for instance, refers to Christian religion.

In any type of retail outlet, people experience a common visual currency or cues due to the way that certain concepts have been repeated by many different products over a number of years. Consumers have thus learned to interpret some symbols featured on products inside a supermarket in a certain way, in addition to their ability to recognise symbols from the wider common visual currency of society. This common currency may make a person associate a cow icon with milk, an apple with fruit, or a football with sport. Packaging designers use such visual currency to provide consumers with instantly recognisable insights into the nature or quality of a product.

Torres Sangre de Toro Tinto Crianza

Shown below is a detail from the branding for Torres Sangre de Toro red wine, which uses the symbolism of the bull to create a strong image. The bull is an icon that represents Spain, the origin of the wine, and is treated here with a certain degree of humour – the bull is presented lying down and just taking it easy.

Fleriana

Greek design agency Mouse created the packaging shown here for the brand Fleriana. The packaging features an image of a tailor's dummy covered with flowers as a visual shorthand to indicate that the products are 100 per cent natural. The Fleriana design narrates a natural story, using elegance as its differentiating characteristic and descriptive symbolism to suggest a friendly product.

< Key text   **Visual shorthand**   Branding, language and colour >

Different types of symbols

A symbol is a pictorial element that communicates a concept, idea or object. Symbols include letters that refer to spoken sounds, road signs and flags. Different types of symbols can be used to effectively communicate the same concept. The main types of symbols are explored below.

Symbol

A representation of a concept, object or action. A flag, for example, is a symbol. It doesn't look like the country that it represents, but through common agreement, we are able to make the connection.

Icon

An icon is a graphic element that represents an object, person or something else by reducing it to simple and instantly recognisable characteristics. A smiley face is an icon, for example, as it still looks like a face.

Indexes

Indexes are something that guide or otherwise serve as a reference to something else. A milk churn is an index of cheese, for example.

Degrees of abstraction

A symbol is often an abstract representation of an object. A designer can use various degrees of abstraction to take the symbol further away from a realistic representation of the actual object, yet make it more representative at the same time. The ability to visually abstract enables a designer to focus on and convey a succinct message that successfully creates associations to the product. Thus, a designer can focus on the value that a product will have for consumers rather than on its physical characteristics, which may not be easy to transmit. The more abstract the image, however, the more tenuous the link becomes until it reaches the point when it is lost altogether. There is a balance between creating something interesting yet simple enough to be understood.

Symbols in relation to placement

Symbols and their meanings are not fixed and are often provided through their placement. The image of a cow, for example, would have a different meaning in a food store than in a furniture store, where it may index leather rather than cheese. We need to consider how people may interpret symbols when they are placed in different contexts, as these interpretations may not be what you would anticipate or desire.

Tesco cheese

This cheese packaging by R Design for Tesco is lighthearted and communicates a sense of fun, with the cow looking over the fence towards the consumer. The cow acts as an index to the product. The packaging also includes flag symbols to represent the country of origin of each cheese, be that the Republic of Ireland or Scotland, as in the examples presented above.

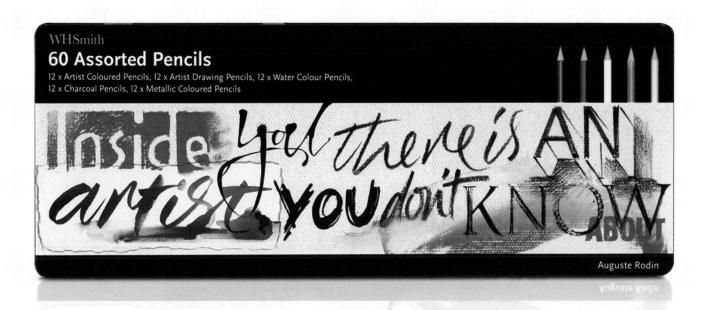

WHSmith
60 Assorted Pencils
12 x Artist Coloured Pencils, 12 x Artist Drawing Pencils, 12 x Water Colour Pencils,
12 x Charcoal Pencils, 12 x Metallic Coloured Pencils

Auguste Rodin

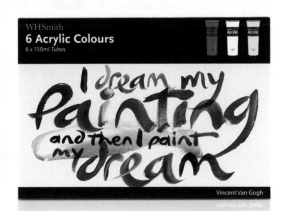

WHSmith
6 Acrylic Colours
6 x 150ml Tubes

Vincent Van Gogh

WHSmith
A4 Sketch Pad with 40 Sheets
110gsm

John Singer Sargent

WHSmith
24 Water Colour Pencils

Vincent Van Gogh

W H Smith

This packaging by R Design for the UK stationers W H Smith features hand-painted, sketched and drawn designs
conveying quotes from several famous artists, including Vincent van Gogh, Auguste Rodin and John Singer Sargent,
which inform potential customers about the creative joys of art. The packaging presents a visual shorthand of what can
potentially be achieved using the products. The designs use an eclectic mix of typefaces as a signifier for creativity.

< Visual shorthand   **Branding, language and colour**   Point of difference >

Branding, language and colour

The approach that a designer chooses to take towards packaging design is largely dominated by the need to procure a positive reaction from the target consumer. Creating packaging with strong appeal requires an understanding of branding, language and colour.

Branding

Branding is often thought of as just a logo or catchy name that has been created for a product, but the concept of what constitutes a brand is actually much broader than this. Branding is the whole process that surrounds the creation of a unique name and image for a product in the consumer's mind, which is presented through advertising campaigns and on packaging materials. The aim of branding is to establish a significant and differentiated position in the market for a product that attracts and retains customers from the target group.

Brands are used to communicate certain attributes or characteristics of a product. Brands may stress high quality, low cost or natural ingredients, that is, intrinsic qualities of the product. They may also emphasise tradition, quality, trust, prestige or experience, elements that refer to the qualities of the company.

In certain product categories, for example bottled water, branding is the main differentiating factor between competing products. For a brand to be successful, the qualities it projects have to be credible and permeate through the entire packaging design, including the outer container, the inner container, the graphics, the quality of materials used and so on.

Brand drivers

A driver is a factor that contributes to the success of a business or brand, and the five key drivers are as follows:

Relevance: this is the point of difference of the product, or what makes the brand viable. This also relates to the extent to which the benefits that the brand claims to offer are credible and believable.

Awareness: are people aware of the brand? Do they know it exists and where they can get it?

Emotional connection: how much is the brand needed by the consumer? Is it essential?

Value: this relates to whether consumers perceive the brand as offering a good combination of goods and services for the price that they will pay; this has implications for pricing strategy and distribution outlets.

Accessibility: how convenient is the brand to purchase? Is it practical to carry?

Brand drivers   *Relevance*   *Awareness*   *Emotion*   *Value*   *Accessibility*

The five drivers of branding: these can fundamentally contribute to the success of any given business or brand.

Gee Beauty

The Canadian design agency GJP Advertising designed packaging for various products created by Gee Beauty, shown here. The visual approach is dominated by humorous texts set in large-scale typography within white space to convey the brand message. The neutral colouration and photographic styling combine to add elegance to the brand.

Hello, Handsome.

Darling, we love your strength of character & rugged nature. But even Clint Eastwood (in that Western you love so much) enjoyed a cut & polish after he shot half the townsfolk. So there's no reason why you should be left to fend for yourself. Our line of male products & services separate the men from the boys - smoothing out the rough edges while keeping your charm & character intact. There will be plenty of time to save the world, so let it go. Visit geebeauty.com

Stay Gorgeous.

Life is too short not to look drop dead gorgeous. You have the time, whether you know it or not. Let us show you how to take advantage of a brow shaping, a divinely quick skin treatment or the ever-popular buff & polish. You're in, you're out. You're gorgeous. It's that simple. Visit geebeauty.com before you slip out the door.

Curves ahead

An essential tool for curling your lashes for more definition. Give them body, give them volume. Because they ask so little in return.

Inside every worn down pencil is a point, dying to be sharp

Won't you please make her wish come true. You won't be sorry.

Language

Language is used to communicate ideas succinctly, a fact that packaging design exploits to inform potential customers of why they should purchase a given product. Consumers typically spend mere seconds looking at a product on a shelf, so communication has to be instant and easy to grasp. Language is perhaps the most important aspect to get right when developing a new brand as the written information on a package will project a tone of voice or attitude that must be consistent with the brand concept. The variety and flexibility of language provides many tools for the designer and copywriter to use when creating brands and packaging. Below are some 'tools' used in brand name generation.

Synonyms

A synonym is a word that has the same or nearly the same meaning as another word or other words in a language. Large, great and grand are all synonyms for something of big stature. New products are often named to differentiate them from those that currently exist. Successful products that create new categories sometimes end up becoming the name that describes the product; 'Hoover' is synonymous for vacuum cleaner and 'iPod' a catch-all word for electronic music file-players generally.

Portmanteaux

Portmanteau words are those whose meaning is derived from a blending of two or more distinct words. One example is the portmanteau of 'elle' and 'vive' used by haircare products brand Elvive, which communicates that the products are for women and rejuvenate hair (the word 'elle' means 'she' and 'vive' means 'lives' in French). Brand name portmanteaux enable two different concepts to be communicated simultaneously in the limited space that packaging provides.

Phonetics

Some brand names are formed from a phonetic combination of syllables that simply sound nice and which encapsulate the idea of a product rather than being 'real' words. Others are created from an intentional syllabic mis-spelling of a word. Weetabix,

for example, is a phonetic mis-spelling and portmanteau of the words 'wheat' and 'biscuits'. The original product name was actually 'Weet-Bix', a portmanteau that was modified by the addition of an 'a', resulting in a name that rolls off the tongue. Another example is the phonetic mis-spelling that adapts the words 'brilliant' and 'cream' into 'Brylcreem', a name that conveys two key qualities of the hairstyling brand product: that it gives hair a brilliant shine and is a cream. Many successful brand names feature three–four syllables and many use combinations of the 'CV syllable', whereby a single consonant is followed by a vowel, as with Coca-Cola.

Names

Using a real or imaginary name can lend a brand a sense of heritage and prestige, giving the product a 'personal' seal of approval. Young's beer and McCoy's crisps give the impression that Young's is an authority on brewing beer and that McCoy's is an expert at making crisps. Often, this type of branding will manifest itself as a signature, which acts as a signifier to the authenticity of the product. This is discussed further on pages 112–115.

Alliteration

Alliterations are patterns of consonants that start words and form memorable phonetic patterns; such as Coca-Cola, Dunkin' Donuts, and Nobby's Nuts.

Tone of voice

This helps to establish the structure of the relationship between a brand and consumers. Medicinal, health care and technical products tend to use an authoritative tone of voice that reassures consumers and establishes trust, for example. The aspirin brand name Anadin sounds direct, firm and authoritative; whereas Colombian ice pop Bon Bon Ice sounds light-hearted, informal and fun.

Cultural and linguistic differences

A brand name may not always work or translate well in a different geographic region. Haircare products brand Schwarzkopf maintains its German name in English-speaking markets as the English translation of the word – 'blackhead' – has the negative connotation of oily skin.

Cocopia

R Design's packaging for luxury chocolates brand Cocopia (left) features a brand name that is a portmanteau of coco and utopia.

Froosh

This identity, created by Pearlfisher for Swedish urban smoothie brand Froosh, features bottle graphics that create clear on-shelf differentiation for the five product varieties. Each label has a colour palette that makes simple and effective use of contrast and includes a strapline statement that speaks directly to the consumer, visually and verbally reinforcing the brand's no-nonsense approach. The Froosh logo converts the double 'o' of the name into a fruit motif that also adds a twist of humour.

< Visual shorthand **Branding, language and colour** Point of difference >

Help Remedies

This packaging created by Little Fury for over-the-counter healthcare products brand Help Remedies features a custom logotype and a friendly, straightforward, colour-coded packaging system that ensures that each product line reflects the company's mission to make health issues simple.

Colour

Colour is an essential part of branding and establishing the brand statement. Colour decisions have to take into account the colours used by competitors and whether the aim is to fit in or stand out. The power of colour is important for brand recognition as consumers often use it as a short cut when purchasing products; they will often look for a familiar red and yellow bottle, for example, rather than read the labels of products on the shelf. It is for this reason that 'me-too' brands often feature labels in similar colours to the market leader in order to benefit from such familiar associations.

The effective use of colour in packaging design can be a highly involved decision due to the various connotations, associations and messages that colours can send out. Colour meanings are wide and varied and, perhaps most significantly, they are also culturally dependent. Certain packaging colours refer to particular tastes or qualities, with pink and red indicating sweetness for example, while white and blue suggest purity and refinement. The colour green typically refers to mint flavouring or organic produce, while to attract attention to 'new' or 'improved' products or formulas, designers frequently use red and yellow.

Using colour

Colour can also be used by manufacturers to plant specific ideas about their products in the minds of consumers; for example, by using white and blue to suggest the freshness and purity of white flour and sugar. The use of red may indicate a powerful product, to indicate the strength of a domestic bleach, for example. Orange and yellow are used on packaging for cereals and vitamins to convey the healthy energy that such products are designed to provide to consumers.

Colour communicates information about who a product is aimed at or about its fabrication. Purple, gold and black indicate exclusivity, expensiveness, luxury and quality in certain product segments, while blues tend to convey a sense of tradition, conservativeness and reliability. The use of colour concepts for brands extends to the colouration of the product itself, even for comestible items where food colourants are used. This results in peas that are bright green and tomatoes that are bright red because such vivid colouring is perceived as indicating that the food is more ripe and healthy, even if it is less flavourful. A more intense hue is also thought to show that the product is of a higher quality.

One aspect that is essential for the use of colour in packaging is that colour reproduction has to be exact and consistent, particularly regarding the depth of colour. Colour changes may result in the mistaken belief that a product has been on the shelf for a long time or that the product quality is variable.

Common colour associations

The list below shows some of the common associations attached to different colours in the Western world.

White: Purity, innocence, optimism.
Silver: Peace, tenacity.
Grey: Stability.
Yellow: Intelligence, innovation, optimism, precaution. Gives sensation of freshness in retail environments.
Gold: Strength, luxury.
Orange: Energy.
Red: Vitality, power, passion, aggression.
Purple: Serenity, luxury, mourning.
Blue: Truth, serenity, harmony, fidelity, responsibility, tradition. The least appealing colour for food due to links with toxic or spoiled substances (blue, black or purple).
Green: Moderation, equilibrium, tradition, ecological, minty taste.
Black: Silence, power, elegance, sadness.

When designing or thinking about brands that are going to be globally manufactured and distributed, including within eastern cultures, you need to consider any specific connotations that colour may convey in different cultural environments. For example, in Western cultures, black and purple are typically colours of mourning, whereas in Eastern cultures this emotional state is largely represented by the colour white.

Selecting colours

Different methods are available for selecting compatible colour combinations, rather than merely relying on guesswork or using trial and error. As a starting point, a designer can base colour choice decisions on colour psychology and the cultural meanings that colours have, as discussed above.

Colour selection can also be aided by tools such as colour wheels. The wheel has warm colours such as reds and oranges, and cool colours such as blues. The colour wheel allows a designer to deconstruct the colour structure used by competing brands and then make the decision of whether to choose something similar or opt for something completely different, to zig or to zag. For example, if brands A, B and C feature colours from one part of the wheel, you might choose colours for brand D from the opposite side in order to thereby differentiate it. A colour wheel allows you to 'place' competitors by colour, to show where gaps exist and also where possible niches can be found. Although there are potentially millions of colour combinations at your disposal, you will be surprised at how many have already been used!

< Branding, language and colour   **Point of difference**   Personality >

Point of difference

One of packaging's key roles is to establish a point of difference from competing products by highlighting and communicating a credible difference based on a significant product characteristic.

Packaging is the difference

A product has many different attributes, including the quality and source of its ingredients or materials, the quality of its design and manufacture, its longevity and robustness, its style or aesthetic qualities, its cost, its size and so on. But what is a product's point of difference? In many instances, such as with sugar, milk or cosmetics, a product will not be noticeably different from its competitors. One product may be virtually indistinguishable from another and few possess a unique selling point, such as deodorants, for example, although each marketer claims that their product does. Without the branded packaging, or the 'clothes' that the product wears, it would be hard or even impossible to tell one product from another. Branding helps consumers distinguish one white T-shirt from another. Packaging design often focuses on creating a point of difference so that buyers can differentiate products, form opinions and establish preferences that will lead to purchase decisions.

Packaging design is also a product attribute, is often the point of difference between brands and is the mechanism through which a consumer differentiates one from another. It is also the way in which consumers express personal preferences and establish emotional connections to particular products. Packaging can be varied to present different characteristics to the consumer such as light, heavy, recyclable, non-recyclable, high quality or value.

The rational and the emotional

Different brands have rational, physical differences, such as their quality, colour, smell or feel, which relates to physical product attributes resulting from their ingredients and manufacture. For many products, the real point of difference in a consumer's mind is based upon how they feel about a particular brand rather than on its actual physical composition. This emotional aspect of a brand most often influences people's key buying decisions. Any shampoo will clean hair; but it is branded packaging that leads buyers to think of some shampoos as being environmentally friendly, sensitive to the skin, feminine or masculine, or as luxury or value products.

Brand designers use packaging design to establish and project positive qualities that consumers will establish emotional connections to; for example, by creating the impression that a product is eco-friendly or of superior quality. This could be as simple as showing images relating to a product's strongest attributes or providing a basis for establishing an emotional connection.

Zigging and zagging

Branders often stick close to what the market leader does as it has a tried-and-tested method that has met with success and which in extreme cases can result in trademark infringement. But creating a brand that stands out may make a product uniquely recognisable. This might be achieved by using impactful icons, a unique shape, taking possession of a particular colour or having a logo that creates 'visual equity', for example.

Packaging features a hierarchy of information that has to quickly communicate the key benefit of a product, whether that is taste, value, longevity or something else. Other information is presented in order of importance and it is a legal requirement to present certain other information about a product. A designer also needs to consider functional aspects of packaging and how this fits with the overall product offer. Innovations can increase the importance of packaging to a brand and become part of a product offering, as well as being a point of differentiation. However, innovations can be copied and adopted by competitors, and often are.

USP and ESP

When products are clearly different it is possible to find a real and tangible difference: their unique selling points (USP). However, products that are similar or with slight differences rely on their created emotional selling point or differences (ESP) to become their selling point. Question whether there is a real difference between competing products or whether it will need to be created.

Here! Sod

This unusual range of T-shirts was created by Thai design agency Prompt Design for the opening of Here! Sod, a new online gift outlet. The T-shirts feature images of products typically found in a supermarket and are packaged using a *trompe l'oeil* effect so as to appear to be the actual packaged products, creating a distinctive point of difference.

< Branding, language and colour   **Point of difference**   Personality >

Kalb-Reduktion
Réduction de veau

Apéro-Kürbiskerne
Graine de courge apér

Mandeltuille
Tuile d'amande

Tomatenmojo
Mojo de tomates

Schwarze Nüsse
Noix noires de Pécan

Peperoniconfit
Piment confit

Safranessenz
Essence au safran

Schokococo-Tuille

Apéro-Sonnenblumenker
Graine de tournesol apé

Tomatenessenz
Essence de tomates

Zitronenconfit
Citron confit

Andreas Caminada

The packaging shown here was created by Remo Caminada for a range
of chutneys by the Swiss chef Andreas Caminada. The designs feature
a minimalist intervention on the product's label that creates a point of
difference. Instead of a label containing various facts that covers a large
part of the container's surface, there is just the logo and an expanse
of exposed glass that allows the consumer a complete view of the
contents. Product information is presented on the box together with
a highly noticeable iconic image.

< Point of difference   **Personality**   Persuasion >

Personality

Brands are often developed to have a personality that represents the combined qualities, values or attributes of a product. Establishing a brand personality can be an effective way to communicate product attributes or qualities, particularly for consumer products. Brand personalities can help to establish a variety of emotional connections and relationships to a product, including trust, tradition, joviality or seriousness.

Appealing to hearts and minds

The successful development of an attractive brand personality can differentiate a product from its competitors, particularly in the highly competitive food sector where brands compete with generic 'me-too' products, own brands and national brands. Brand personalities are developed to help establish a bond of trust with consumers and have the ability to transform a product into something that people develop an emotional relationship towards, especially if it is connected with the owner or creator of the product.

Consumers tend to trust people more than faceless corporations or brands, even if the personality they are connecting with is a marketing fabrication, so developing a brand personality can be a very successful strategy if it resonates with issues that people care about and genuinely appeals to their hearts and minds. Brand personalities may focus on a company's long tradition of producing a product, as with the Quaker brand, which is tied into the traits of fair business and quality that the Quakers are noted for. The brand actually has nothing to do with the Quakers but it employs this fictitious brand personality to benefit from associations this may confer.

Burt's Bees

The packaging for Burt's Bees uses the name of company founder, Burt Shavitz, to introduce an element of trust to its range of natural products made with beeswax extracts. Consumers are increasingly sceptical of products made by multinational cosmetic companies and favour the more wholesome values of smaller businesses.

Rellana Hair

Pictured here is packaging for wool created by Ogilvy & Mather Frankfurt for Rellana Hair for its range of fringed yarn. The packaging design creates brand personality through the use of the faces printed onto the label bands of the wool balls whereby the wool becomes hair and beards. This presentation demonstrates the character of the wool at first sight in a cost effective manner and communicates that the wool is perfect for scarves and hats.

< Point of difference   **Personality**   Persuasion >

Literal personality

Brand personalities can be literal, too. Literal brand personalities are those that seek to use the attributes and characteristics of actual people, usually those with a high public profile. The number of literal brand personalities that appear before consumers has increased in recent years as public figures seek to capitalise on their fame in order to earn royalties from product sales. However, some literal personalities aim to draw people to their products for motives other than personal gain, such as for charitable causes, or to promote healthy lifestyles or environmental awareness, for example.

Paul Newman

Newman's Own was an early usage of the literal personality and dates back to 1982. Actor Paul Newman realised that using his image could help raise money for good causes and the company donates all profits to charity.

Levi Roots

This package for Reggae Reggae sauce features a silhouette of its creator, reggae musician and chef Levi Roots. The packaging also reflects the trends of its time: the iPod generation and multiculturalism.

Caesar Cardini

An Italian-born Mexican, Caesar Cardini was the inventor of the infamous Caesar salad. The use of this literal personality stamps the ranch dressing product with both authenticity and originality.

Imagined history

A brand personality begins to generate an imagined history after several years of successfully delivering what the brand promises. Brand managers use this history to show and remind consumers of the brand's longevity and to indicate that the product has effectively become a trusted friend of the family as with, for example, Uncle Ben's or Quaker Oats.

Loyd Grossman
Loyd Grossman foods and sauces are inspired by the travels of the Anglo-American TV chef and critic in the famous food capitals of the world. The literal personality is here used to attract fans of his television shows.

Jamie Oliver
Jamie Oliver is a British TV chef who has become widely known for simple cooking and for helping to reignite interest in food amongst both children and adults in Great Britain and around the world.

Uncle Ben's
A brand like Uncle Ben's has reflected changes in wider social conditions and concerns; the image of 'Uncle Ben' has developed from that of farm worker to board member during the product's history.

< Personality   **Persuasion**   Humour and appropriation >

Persuasion

One of the main functions of packaging design is to help a person make a buying decision. In this role, packaging aims to focus the positive aspects of a product into something that is irresistible to the consumer so persuading them to purchase. Packaging presents various pieces of information, often combined with the strong use of colour and images, to win over the consumer.

Rhetoric

There any many persuasive communication tools that designers can use in packaging design and the majority of these can be found within the principles of rhetoric, the ancient art of discourse that is concerned with using language to communicate effectively. Rhetoric has five canons – *invention* or *discovery*, *arrangement*, *style*, *memory* and *delivery* – each of which can be used within packaging design to optimise the delivery of a message to a particular audience. A discourse often makes use of *logos*, *pathos* and *ethos* to engage an audience and elicit a particular response.

Classical rhetoric trained people to be effective persuaders in public forums and institutions, using language skills to impress their point or position. Today, rhetoric is used by various professions, including journalism, public relations and marketing.

Packaging design frequently uses the rhetorical toolbox to establish a connection with a target audience and to appeal to different aspects of their personality. In general terms, applying the five canons of rhetoric to packaging design can help to form a message that will resonate with the audience through the way it is presented and the narrative created through it. The arrangement, style and delivery of the message are determined by characteristics that it is known that the target group will respond to. Packaging design communication can be made more specific by using some of the other rhetorical skills, explored further here.

Logos, which means persuasion by demonstration of logical proof, real or apparent, can be seen in designs that communicate how exactly a product is better than its competitors, be that because it is stronger, longer lasting, better value, or of superior quality.

Pathos refers to the means of persuasion that appeals to the audience's emotions and sympathies and is used to create emotional connections to a product, often when there is little rational or real difference between products, or where the rational points of differentiation are unlikely to be understood. Use of pathos ranges from the presentation of cute puppies on toilet-paper brand packaging and smiling babies to promote the importance of insurance products, to shock tactics highlighting the grave consequences that may ensue if you do not use a given product. Many health products use pathos in their brand packaging.

Ethos is persuasive appeal based on the character or projected character of the speaker or writer and is one of the reasons that brand managers seek to develop a brand personality that links well with consumers' self-perceptions. The use of ethos can also be seen every time that a star or expert is used to endorse a product, either to project their particular unique abilities onto the product, and by proxy the consumer, or by extending their apparent celebrity 'cool' factor.

Draculis

Greek design agency Mouse created the packaging above for Draculis, a company who produce coffee in bags. The design's intention is to bring visibility to and differentiate the brand from the duopoly of the leading coffee brands. The result is an appetising coffee cup set against a simple black background to imply the full taste of the coffee and the use of letters from the Greek alphabet as initials for each coffee type.

Vitamin Well

The packaging redesign below was created by Swedish design agency Neumeister for health drink Vitamin Well and features the use of logos in its communication. It provides a high degree of clarity with a label that states exactly what the product is for, a text hierarchy displaying the different levels of information and no other visual components.

< Persuasion   **Humour and appropriation**   Protection, attributes and experience >

Humour and appropriation
Through the use of humour, an event, situation or phrase may provoke a feeling of fun, amusement or laughter in others.

Funny weird or funny ha ha?
Through the use of humour, marketers seek to lock a product or brand into the consciousness of a consumer in such a way that they can recognise it more easily when it occurs within the retail environment. Humour is used to aid product recall by consumers by establishing a connection to the product based on the pleasant experience that the humour provoked.

What people consider to be humorous is very subjective. This means that using it can help a message to be effectively delivered directly to a specific group of people, a target group that is likely to recognise and appreciate the particular piece of humour. Humour in design is often structured so that the target group is able to decipher and understand a message whilst people outside the target group are not, or so that it is not important if they do get the joke or not.

Poor use of humour may miss the target group completely or even produce an adverse reaction by being misunderstood or taken out of context; so humour must be used with care as part of a design or brand statement.

Humour does not have to produce a response of side-splitting laughter to be effective. Instead, provoking a slight smile or a brightening of the eyes through a subtle piece of humour may be more effective, such as that employed by the examples pictured on the facing page. Simple graphic devices can provide a humorous twist to what may otherwise be a rather mundane product presentation and can set the viewer the mental challenge of decoding them in order to understand the real meaning behind a product's brand message.

Formalising humour
The power of humour is not to be understated as it goes beyond the mere telling of a joke. Humour has been used as a learning aid for a very long time and is extensively used in advertising to establish a connection with people. The types of humour typically used in design are explored in detail below:

1 *Comparison* involves comparing a product to something it obviously is not.
2 *Personification* is when a humorous brand personality is created that represents the product.
3 *Exaggeration* is to overstate and magnify something out of all proportion, such as Carlsberg's claim to be 'probably the best lager in the world'.
4 *Addition* refers to adding an element that changes the meaning of an item.
5 *Subtraction* is a term used to describe playing up the fact of what a product is *not*, as with the UK dairy-spread brand, I Can't Believe It's Not Butter!
6 *Puns* – using the product as part of a visual pun can produce a humorous twist.
7 *Substitution* is when the product is used as a substitute for something it obviously is not.
8 *Homage* involves putting a humorous spin on something familiar, such as using reference points from art and history.
9 *Trompe l'oeil* literally means 'trick of the eye' and refers to the meeting of the fake and the real. It may be used to make packaging look like a product, such as by making a box of bin liners appear in the shape of a bin, for instance.

Sugarillos
Greek design agency Mouse created the packaging shown left for individual sugar portions produced by Sugarillos. The design features a range of different teaspoons on the packets as a literal interpretation of the pack content: one spoonful of sugar. The design is straightforward and simple but with a decorative element.

Superdrug

Created by burst* for a line of skincare face mask products for the
UK retail chemist Superdrug, this design (right, and below) features
the use of unexpected humour to good effect. The packaging features
a black-and-white image of a woman with the product's constituent
ingredients picked out in colour. The fruit is squished onto the woman's
nose in such a way that it appears like a clown's nose. The model and
the ingredients were shot separately but retouched together so that
they appear as though squeezed onto the model's nose. The image was
positioned so that it wraps around the sachet with the model's open eye
appearing on the back of the packet and the winking eye shown on the
front. The final packaging is irreverent, fun and distinctive.

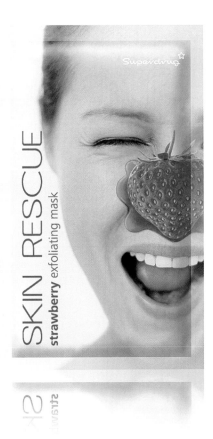  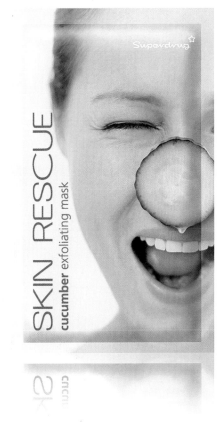

Mint crisps

Here, a coffee cup has been substituted by mints – expressing the link
between them, that is, you eat the mints while drinking coffee (left).
The colour usage of dark green conveys a sense of the flavour (mint and
chocolate) but also of time, as you'd normally expect to eat them in the
evening. R Design's concept is both informative and imaginative.

< Humour and appropriation   **Protection, attributes and experience**   Case study >

Protection, attributes and experience
The primary role that packaging serves is to protect the product that it carries. A cardboard box protects cereal, a bottle protects wine and plastic protects against the ingress or egress of moisture. The type and amount of protection that packaging offers can vary greatly, and there are always cost elements involved. Different materials can be used to protect a product and the branding statement influences which are used.

Protection
Products need protecting from light, moisture, heat, cold, insects, mould, acids, oils, handling, transportation and other environmental hazards. A single-use product will only need protecting once, whereas multi-use products need to consider the product's longer life. Protection considerations also take into account various consumer needs and the changing nature of the retail experience. Traditionally, people bought local, fresh produce and went to the grocery store, butcher's or baker's with a basket to put their goods in. Products had very little protective packaging, in some cases perhaps only a paper bag, or would be placed directly into the shopping basket without further wrapping.

Nowadays, most people shop in supermarkets that have extensive distribution chains and bring products from far and wide around the globe. Products are packaged to protect them from the logistics chain and to facilitate in-store handling and display. As a consequence, we now commonly buy fruit and meat in styrofoam trays that are covered with cling film.

Bell TV
lg2boutique's packaging for Bell TV and Internet products exceeds the protective function of the corrugated board container. Instead of something dull and routine, there are images of people expressing a wide range of emotions, including surprise, enthusiasm, pleasure and amazement at the advantages that Bell products bring to consumers. The faces were printed on white top liner, a material that can reproduce high-quality colour images. This is a packaging attribute that goes beyond the primary protection need and creates a sense of experience. To further reduce Bell TV's environmental footprint, the packaging was created with a carry handle so that the products do not require a bag.

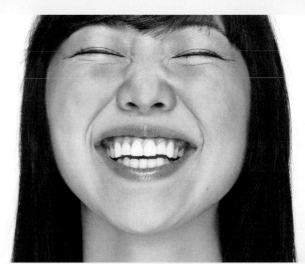

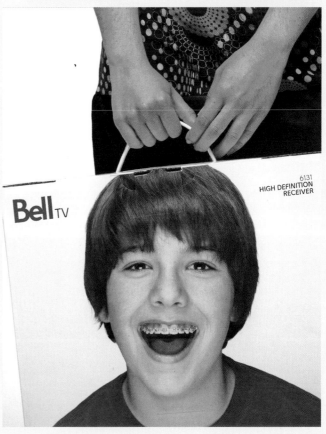

< Humour and appropriation   **Protection, attributes and experience**   Case study >

Types of materials

Materials science continues to add to the wide variety of materials that packaging can be made from via the invention of different composites that provide an increasing array of functionality. Packaging materials have evolved a long way from corrugated cardboard boxes and glass bottles to include thin form plastics and metals, and foil laminate Tetra Paks, amongst other innovations. The primary physical function of any packaging material is to contain and protect a product from different influences such as oxygen, light and moisture. But as markets have become increasingly competitive, the need for packaging to actively promote a brand has grown too. The choice of packaging materials affects overall product weight and therefore shipping costs, while different protective capabilities can prove the defining factor in whether an item is transported successfully or arrives at its destination in pieces.

Groups of materials

Packaging materials can be grouped in many ways, such as by material, function and recyclability.

Flexible

Flexible packaging is used where achieving a lightweight product is more important than the need to protect it against physical shock. Products contained in flexible packaging are often packed within another form of outer packing to provide physical protection during shipping. Examples include aluminium cans, films, carton and board, brick carton and various types of plastic.

Rigid

Rigid packaging materials are those whose primary function is to act as a physical protective barrier that will not deform under pressure or when receiving a certain level of physical shock. Examples include steel cans, glass bottles, HDPE plastics and ceramics.

Plastic

Perhaps the most common packaging material of all due to its ability to be moulded into a wide variety of shapes.

Plastics are light, strong, cheap to manufacture and have a range of protective properties. Yet, they are one of the most difficult packaging materials to recycle and dispose of; they are bulky, degrade slowly and they contaminate.

Metal

Metals are a strong and cheap material, widely used in food and drinks packaging. Tin plate used for canned goods is actually steel covered with tin to prevent oxidisation or rusting. Steel is relatively simple to recycle, while aluminium requires a lot of energy to produce.

Brick carton

Brick carton, such as Tetra Pak, is a light, strong air-tight packaging material that is ideal for the transportation and storage of liquids, such as milk, as it features different layers of plastic and paper aluminium that keep it watertight. Its multi-layer composition makes it more difficult to recycle, however.

Cardboard

Cardboard includes a range of heavy-duty paper products with different grades and performance capabilities used for different packaging functions. From containing individual products using card stock, to corrugated boxes or container board that hold many products, cardboards are easy to recycle and re-use.

Glass

An ideal material for foods, such as liquids, it can be moulded into many different forms, but it is heavier than plastic and its breakage can create potential dangers for users. Glass is easily recyclable.

Films

Various film plastics are used in packaging. Shrink wrap is used where tamper protection is a high priority, such as for DVDs. After an item is wrapped, heat is applied to make the wrap shrink to fit. Cling film is often used to contain and enclose fresh produce in a container.

Pure Land

Shown here is packaging created by Czech Republic design firm Creasence for the Pure Land brand of quails eggs. The packaging features the use of transparent materials that allow the customer to see the product and therefore know when the eggs are running out.

Lokale Helter

This pizza packaging was created by Strømme Throndsen Design for Natural A/S for the Norwegian pizza brand Lokale Helter. The design won the 2009 Good Design Award from The Chicago Athenaeum in the graphics/identity/branding section. The circular card container protects the pizza while creating a strong brand identity based around the highly visible brand name. The packaging does not fully surround the contents but remains open at the sides, making the pizza easy to remove without risk of breakage.

< Humour and appropriation   **Protection, attributes and experience**   Case study >

Attributes

The previous section looked at the protection element of packaging design. Protection is a primary packaging function but it is usually a product's *attributes* that we buy into, rather than how well it is protected. When we purchase a product, we not only buy a physical commodity, such as a bottle of shampoo, but we also buy the promise of that product, that is what it will do for us and how it will make us feel. The promise of the product is a combination of characteristics that are presented to the consumer and augmented through branding. This section explores some of the issues that arise in relation to a product's attributes.

Attribute projection

A product has many different attributes, including the quality and source of its ingredients or materials, the quality of its design and manufacture, its longevity and robustness, its style or aesthetic qualities, its cost, its size and so on. The packaging that a product is contained in can also be viewed as one of its attributes, as this may be attractive, unattractive, light, heavy, recyclable, non-recyclable and so on.

Branded packaging seeks to reflect the positive and desirable qualities of the product via the packaging materials. This could be as simple as showing images relating to its strongest attributes or replicating and mirroring some of these, for example by using similar materials in the packaging. The packaging design should include some of the key brand attributes identified during the research stage and developed in the design concept.

Materials as experience

The choice of materials helps to create and define the user experience, such as by providing smooth or tactile surfaces to interact with, or different things to pull, tug or hold. Packaging is a three-dimensional creation and so designers can explore shape creation as part of the design process to produce something that goes beyond a two-dimensional image. It may also be possible to use a means of opening a package that adds a distinctive element and unique experience to using a product.

Larynn, London

Z3 Design created these packaging designs for the Crystalline range of cosmetic products by Larynn, London. Each product is named after a different crystal (pictured here are sapphire (middle), diamond (top) and ruby (bottom)), and the packaging design is based around the range name. The design tends towards cool and clear qualities, rather than the emotive attributes that other cosmetic products often base their brand designs upon.

New You

Shown here is the artwork for a record cover created by Contentismissing Studio for the *New You* EP by duo Eve White that features male and female dancers that the listener can put together. The design translates the concept of a child's jumping-jack into something more sexy, club-like and ironic by splitting the jumping-jack into individual parts, from which the listener can put together their 'new you'.

< Humour and appropriation   **Protection, attributes and experience**   Case study >

Experience

Experience focuses on a person's physical interaction with a package, its ease of use and its tactile qualities, and how this adds to the story about a product. In most instances, it is important for a package to be easy to open, although not in all cases – for example, this is not the case with safety lids on medicine bottles which are designed precisely to prevent children from opening them. Ease of access has to be geared to the product type, and also to the kind of interactive experience desired for the consumer.

Creating interest

Creating an interesting or memorable packaging experience can add value to a brand and help with its positioning in the mind of a consumer. The quality of this experience can enhance and further the brand characteristics of a product. At the very least, the packaging experience should be consistent with the branding and not detract from it. For example, if a product is being positioned as exclusive or luxurious, it should have packaging that reinforces this. Perfume packaging attempts to do this through the use of glass bottles, rather than plastic ones, formed in intricate shapes that create a physical experience for the user when they are handled.

Boa Boca Gourmet

Pictured (below) are images of the Feitoàmao range of products created by Policarpo Design in Portugal for food products firm, Boa Boca Gourmet. The design features an innovative touch as the packages of dried fruit and nut combinations are created to be split open at the centre, whereby each half contains a separate product.

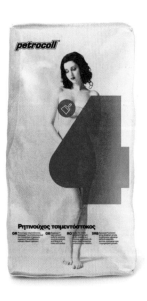

Petrocoll

Shown (left) is award-winning packaging created by Greek design agency Mouse for Petrocoll's cement bags and putty products. The products are presented like any fast moving consumer good to differentiate the brand from its competition. Aimed at construction workers, the design employed non-provocative female figures as a way of creating a buzz on the typical construction site, with each figure dressed in clothing with various degrees of transparency to subtly communicate the product characteristics.

HEMA markers and pencils

The packaging for markers and pencil products created by Studio Kluif for European retailer Hema shown here feature a die-cut that the design team were not permitted to change. They turned this restriction into a benefit by incorporating it into the design via a series of illustrations of monsters, robots and fantasy animals. The product forms the main focus of the packaging and the unique combination of illustration and product triggers the imagination of the young target user.

< Humour and appropriation   Protection, attributes and experience   Case study >

A sense of ritual

Designers need to understand how people use products and the rituals they perform when doing so in order to make packaging that meets or enhances their expectations. Understanding such rituals can shed light on a design problem and identify ways to make a product more appealing to the target audience. Some people make tea using teabags, some use a teapot, while others use a diffuser: each method involves its own ritual. Coffee drinkers may use instant powder, a filter machine, a French press or an espresso machine. Some people grind the coffee beans prior to making the beverage. One thing that many people share in common is the pleasure gained from inhaling the fresh coffee aroma from a newly opened packet.

Packaging can be designed to ease or complement the rituals that people perform when using certain products, and those that do so successfully can help to improve product sales. Personal rituals may also affect material selection. For example, some wine drinkers like the ritual of uncorking a bottle and so will not buy wine with screw-top caps or wine in a carton.

Alternate packaging rituals

Rituals can programme people to act in certain ways with certain products, and to associate specific or particular actions to their usage. But many food products can be presented using alternate packaging methods with different opening mechanisms. For example, food can be packaged in easy-to-open vacuum packs as well as in tin cans. However, usage rituals for preparing certain foods may be so strong and ingrained that a switch to a different packaging method may be met with disapproval and prevent its uptake, even if it offers other advantages over a traditional method.

Packaging innovation may enable new rituals to be developed and become commonplace. Sun blocks and sunscreens are traditionally viscous white substances that stick to your fingers and easily get contaminated with sand. Nowadays, many sunscreens are available in sprays that are easy to apply, do not have the perceived negative attributes of traditional creams, and allow people to create new rituals to give themselves a quick spritz thereby ensuring their protection from the sun. This is one example of the ways in which people can readily adapt to innovative packaging that has been designed to make their lives easier and their use of a given product more manageable.

Cacao

Taxi Studio created this chocolate packaging for Willie's World-Class Cacao, which presents the consumer with a mystery contained in a black paper wrapper detailed with a gold foil block (above). By removing the paper wrapper, a gold block of the foil-wrapped cacao is revealed; this then peels back to present the sculptural block of cacao, which is finished off with a stamp of the company's logo.

Coffee

The vacuum-packed coffee packaging employed by Italian coffee producer Lavazza (above) helps to create a ritual for users, as the vacuum pack presents the coffee as a solid block that softens upon opening, which then releases the distinct aroma that consumers enjoy when preparing the drink.

Champagne

Perhaps the ultimate ritual in food and drink presentation is opening a bottle of champagne (above). Champagne and fizzy wines require a more elaborate corkage system as they ferment in the bottle, producing carbon dioxide (the gas that gives them their fizz). The cork thus needs to be secured by a wire cage so that it does not prematurely pop out. Colour foils are used over the wire cage to improve the visual appearance and enhance the opening ritual.

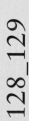

< Protection, attributes and experience   **Case study**   Student exercise >

Case study

Ultrasilencer Special Edition

BVD

Let's take a look at the packaging solution created by the Swedish design agency BVD for the Ultrasilencer Special Edition vacuum cleaner. Designed by Pia Wallén for the domestic appliance and vacuum cleaner manufacturer Electrolux, it formed part of a project to name the product, produce a logo and create the brand, as well as to create the packaging design, promotional material and store presentation material.

BVD was tasked with creating a graphic identity and packaging solution that mirrored designer Pia Wallén's interpretation of the product. Inspired by the quiet sound of falling snow, the solution featured a typographic-based identity that was created and applied directly onto the vacuum cleaner in a light grey tone.

The packaging was turned 'inside-out'; the interior has a white, glossy surface that encases the product, while the exterior is brown from the natural cardboard used. The product name was screen-printed onto the outside of the package in white and orange to create an industrial feel in contrast to the white perfectionism of the vacuum cleaner. Produced in a limited edition of 5,000, The Ultrasilencer sold well; the packaging generated such interest in the product that a waiting list was created. A 20 per cent increase in production costs was compensated for by a 60 per cent increase in retail price, made possible by the quality of the design.

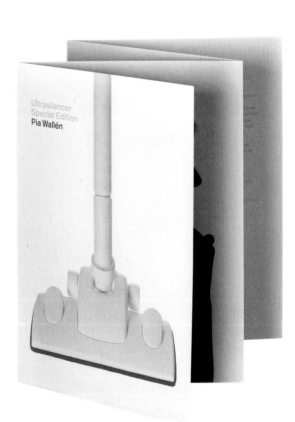

Ultrasilencer
Special Edition
Pia Wallén

...lencer Special Edition Pia Wallén hos
...ckan 18–21.

...tolkning av en av världens tystaste
...te ljud hon känner till – ljudet av fallande
...r i signalorange som suddar ut gränsen
...ux.com/specialedition.

...my Myllymäki. OSA på party@asplund.org

ASPLUND   ⊞ **Electrolux**

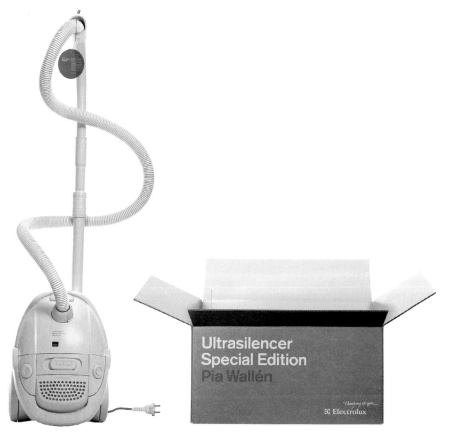

Ultrasilencer
Special Edition
Pia Wallén
⊞ Electrolux

Ultrasilencer
Special Edition
Pia Wallén
⊞ Electrolux

< Case study   **Student exercise**   Chapter 4 >

Student exercise
Ritual

Project set by Nigel Aono-Billson

Lavazza vacuum-packed coffee is a solid block when purchased that softens when opened, releasing the full aroma of the coffee within, thereby creating a sense of ritual for consumers. This packaging was previously explored on page 129.

As we have seen, there are rituals attributed to certain products, as well as to interacting or simply enjoying them. The way in which we engage with a product can lead us to create a daily ritual around their use or to something which becomes symbolic and specifically related to that product and/or event.

For example, the opening of a bottle of champagne often signifies a celebration or important event. The making of tea has special cultural significance, particularly in Japan and China, where tea ceremonies are honorific, not just of the tea, but of life itself.

The aroma of coffee and toast has strong social metaphors in the West. It is only natural to sniff a freshly opened pack of coffee, as it evokes other lifetime experiences, which in turn transmit emotions relating to our daily rituals and behaviour.

As a packaging designer, considering these rituals can inform the way you design. Part of your research should not only be about the product, but also about the activities and rituals surrounding the product. These rituals can provide a rich source of inspiration and information.

Student exercise
How to create a package that has a ritual attached

The item that you are to package or repackage may be at first glance mundane, just a simple household or everyday thing. Alternatively, it may be luxurious, exotic and tantalising. How can you add a ritual aspect or association to it?

1. Create
Choose one of the five senses: sight, sound, taste, touch or smell. Create a new package for either an everyday product or a luxury product, that when used/interacted with has an element of ritual about it. The usage/experience element of the packaging should evoke some aspect of ritualisation through emotion or behaviour. Consider shape, structure, texture and construction when thinking about how to achieve this.

The packaging can be playful but should still retain a brand communication relative to its contents. The resulting design will have visual equity, along with a strong personality and attitude.

You may wish to also consider: national and international trends and communities, differentials between consumer groups, usage and event relationships.

2. Consider:
• its shape, form, size, quantity and volume;
• look at any similar products and brands;
• record all or any similarities and dissimilarities;
• take note of the uniqueness of all colour ways and key colours.

3. Explore
• Look at all existing identities and brands.
• Compare high-quality and low-quality products.
• Study individual packaging structures and associated materials.
• Explore opening procedures and storage.
• Consider associated sensory experiences.

Bibliography and further reading
Grip Design, (2008). *1,000 Package Designs: A Complete Compilation of Creative Containers.* Rockport Publishers.

Hargreaves, B. (2004). *Eat ME: Successful, Seductive Food Packaging Design.* Rotovision.

Mollerup, P. (2006). *Collapsibles: A Design Album of Space-Saving Objects.* Thames & Hudson.

Parsons, T. (2009). *Thinking: Objects – Contemporary Approaches to Product Design.* AVA Publishing.

Pipes, A. (2007). *Drawing for Designers: Drawing skills, Concept sketches, Computer systems, Illustration, Tools and materials, Presentations, Production techniques.* Laurence King Publishing.

Form and elements

This chapter explores the design decisions that lie behind the physical forms and design elements that comprise the packaging of a branded product. The range of different materials that are available to a designer mean that packaging can be made in an incredible array of shapes and forms thus giving a designer ample opportunity to be creative in terms of their materials usage and choices when designing a receptacle to contain or hold a product.

One function of packaging is to act as a surface upon which to apply the text and images of a design. The information to be communicated via packaging is a mixture of statutory information, such as weights and measures; general information, such as ingredients contained within a given product; and information that consumers are increasingly demanding, such as details about the recycled content and recyclability of the packaging, as well as about the ethical credentials of a brand.

Technological progress means that there are many options open to a designer by which high-quality colour graphics can be applied to a container. These processes give a designer greater scope to use photography and illustration to form the elements of a design, and to be more creative and innovative with typography.

Text and graphics not only appear on the front of a package, but are an important element of the reverse of the pack also due to the supplementary and obligatory information that must legally be provided, according to the nature of the product.

'Good design is innovative
Good design makes a product useful
Good design is aesthetic
Good design makes a product understandable
Good design is unobtrusive
Good design is honest
Good design is long-lasting
Good design is thorough, down to the last detail
Good design is environmentally friendly
Good design is as little design as possible.'

Dieter Rams

Ten principles for good design

Dieter Rams

The question of how to select both form and elements when developing a design is really concerned with how a design concept is turned into a reality, and the various decisions about the choice of materials and design elements that are made to enable this. A concept is a general idea that directs the focus of the design effort and it can be interpreted or put into effect in different ways. Selecting the form and elements during the design stage involves the message being crafted using a combination of text, images and illustrations to communicate the overall idea of the concept.

The design of the form and elements may involve generating and testing various communication strategies and techniques before arriving at one that works effectively. As the design is worked up, the concept itself may be further refined and improved as the design team gets a better feel for the job and of how to successfully meet its desired objectives.

Being flexible and creative is paramount for the design team at this stage, in order to produce solutions that remain true to the design concept; as is taking advantage of the many possibilities afforded by the increasing range of materials and image development software available. One abiding sounding board for designers is the ten principles of good design, drawn up by Dieter Rams (facing page). Rams was one of the most influential industrial designers of the twentieth century and head of design at Braun for over 30 years; he once explained his design approach in the phrase 'weniger, aber besser', which freely translates as 'less, but better'.

Pictured (right) is the 606 Universal Shelving system created by Dieter Rams in 1960 for Vitsoe, which was conceived to be both timeless and flexible. The design is kit-based and can be built to serve the specific storage problems of the user, and reflects his working tenet of 'less, but better' in practice. The system is the structure or packaging of the possessions that will be stored within it. Its modularity aims to give users maximum flexibility to create the storage spaces that they need with the appropriate accessories. The design aims to simplify the concept of storage.

Rams' ten principles can readily be adapted to packaging design, as its results are often innovative and make a product useful; packaging can be aesthetic and help us to understand a product, and it should be honest and concerned with the environment. Applying Rams' ten principles will also help to prevent the design from diverging too greatly from the concept.

The issue of whether packaging should be long-lasting and unobtrusive remains open to debate and depends to a large extent on the type of product that is being packaged. Jonathan Sands believes that doing pre-market testing should be considered to ensure that the packaging will find a willing audience; but it may be that consumers never quite know what they are looking for until someone shows them something new.

Looking at what is happening in other markets also serves as a way to pick up on new ideas or different approaches to packaging design. Look at what is happening in Europe, North America or Asia; and, as Sands advises, 'be different and ensure your pack has its own visual equity, a strong personality and attitude.'

This chapter will raise the following questions:
- To what extent should a designer stick to or diverge from the design concept?
- What communications strategies will best meet the needs of the design concept?
- How can symbols or other graphic devices help meet the design goals?

< Key text   Form and design   Shape and ergonomics >

Form and design
A packaged brand is essentially the combination of two distinct parts: its physical *form* and its *design*. Its form concerns its shape and ergonomics, while its design concerns the surface graphics that tell a story to a consumer.

Form
The form of a package is concerned with developing an appropriate shape and use of the necessary materials that will result in the physical functionality required at a cost that is acceptable. Decisions will also need to be taken at this stage about the weight of materials, as different choices will add to or reduce shipping costs, will affect the feel of the product in terms of the tactile sensation given by its materials and finish, and will also impact upon the ergonomics of the finished package in terms of how easy it is to handle, hold and use.

Design
Design aims to tell a story or to establish a narrative for a product in order to generate sufficient appeal that will help to persuade people to buy it. The form of packaging chosen can make a major contribution to such a story, as well as to help establish its parameters and furnish some of its details. The main part of a narrative will be told by the surface graphics, the element that most consumers would generally consider to constitute the design. As we shall explore in this chapter, surface graphics can be used in many ways to both construct and subsequently develop a narrative for the target consumer.

Thinking in three dimensions
Packages typically have a clearly discernible front and back, and this is where most emphasis is placed in terms of design, to ensure that the front presents a good face to the consumer, for example. In reality, packaged items are more complex than this as they have sides, edges, tops and bottoms, all of which offer surfaces for the placement of graphics and information. A designer has to take into account that packaging has three dimensions rather than two, and that containers have a series of 'faces' or flat shapes that can each be equally used to communicate the brand message. Packaging is something that we can hold, handle and explore as we open, close, reseal, empty and refill it. All of the actions that relate to consumer interaction during the product's use need to be considered during its design phase.

Volume
Packaging contains a volume of space; and many different shapes can be created to contain a specific volume. Packaging designers are therefore not limited to using boxes but have the freedom to explore shape and form. Thinking in three dimensions enables designers to be more creative and to use the corners and contours of packaging as live surfaces, rather than viewing them merely as dead areas, and to thereby explore different ways of presenting a brand. When designing product packaging, it is important to make initial mock ups in the form of three-dimensional test versions, which will enable you to see how one face works with the others. What happens to the message when a package is rotated to the back by an end user. Is there message continuity and coherence? How do the sides relate to the front? What is on the top and bottom of the packaging? What is inside the packaging other than the product itself?

Information hierarchies
Deciding on the order of importance, or hierarchy, of product or brand information that will need to be displayed on a product's packaging enables it to be presented or revealed as needed. Too much information presented in the same style or size can be hard to access or digest as the eye struggles to find an entry point. People typically look to the largest image or type first and use this as an entry point, before moving on to information set in increasingly smaller typesizes.

Using a clear and unambiguous hierarchy helps to clarify the brand's position, as a packaged item essentially provides a brand narrative in a similar way to that of a book or a film. The delivery of information also needs to be paced in order to make it easy for consumers to receive and decipher. This is crucial in a fast-paced retail environment as products have to convey important information quickly and in a way that enables them to stand out distinctly from rival competitors.

skintuary

Sanitizing
& Moisturizing
Hand Cream

Crème à main
antiseptique
& hydratante

4-Hour Protection
Protection 4 heures

Kills 99.9% of germs
Tue 99.9% des germes

Alcohol and triclosan free
Sans alcool, sans triclosan

5 Fl OZ/140 ML

ingredients

Vitamin E,
Avocado Oil,
Jojoba Oil &
Grape Seed Oil
Protects &
moisturizes hands
Note: Unscented

Vitamine E,
huile d'avocat,
huile de jojoba
et huile de pépin
de raisin
Protège et hydrate
les mains
Note: Non-parfumé

Skintuary

This packaging is by Canadian design agency Mookai for a new brand of sanitizing hand cream.
The elegant graphic treatment (its design) runs around the outer of the bottle (its form). There is
an overall simplicity to the design, with the front containing information about the product and
the reverse listing its ingredients, blurring the distinction between the front and back of pack,
and creating an interesting distinction of scales of typography. Intended to be sold in upmarket
retailers, the packaging has to both reflect this elegance and impart a feeling of cleanliness.

Shape and ergonomics

There are two main considerations in the design of a physical object, its form or *shape* and the *ergonomics* of that form. The form is what the object looks like and the story that this tells, while its ergonomics consist of how it is designed in order to maximise user efficiency and reduce strain.

Shape and narratives

Packaging can be created in many diverse forms, and its shape used to help tell the narrative that a brand seeks to communicate. With various materials and forming technologies available, designers have a great degree of freedom to create packaging that both physically and aesthetically represents a brand's key characteristics. Packaging can go much further than merely protecting a product and facilitating its physical distribution.

Designers work with brand managers to instil and project the qualities of a brand into its packaging to facilitate the buying decision. Packaging shapes can give a consumer a clear idea of the product narrative, which will be further developed and reinforced by its surface graphics and any information contained in its labeling and brand imagery.

Containers are often shaped to form part of or to harmonise with the brand narrative; for example, curves suggest sensuality, while straight lines suggest modernity. The inspiration for the use of shape in a packaging design can come from historical reference or research, as in the Marmite example shown below, or from unrelated chance as in the Chanel bottle shown on the facing page. The creative use of shape and form helps to differentiate products in a competitive retail environment, particularly for product groups where it may be difficult for a consumer to distinguish one product from another, such as with bottled water, shampoos and cosmetics.

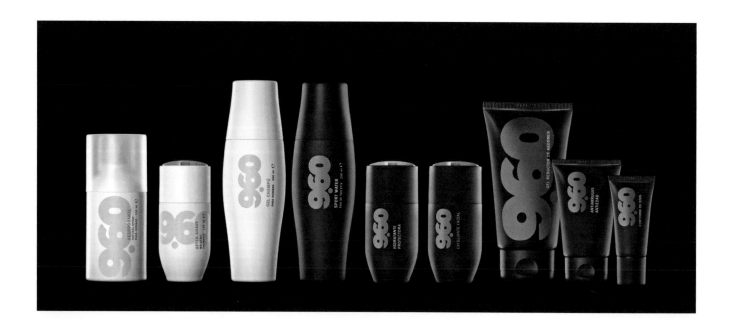

RNB Laboratories

Lavernia & Cienfuegos created this packaging for a mass-market range of male cosmetic products for RNB Laboratories, exclusively distributed in the Spanish supermarket chain Mercadona (shown below and on the facing page). The product line relates to concepts such as being fit, playing sport and exercising, which is reinforced in the packaging through its references to the morphology of human muscles. All of the 100ml and 200ml containers are designed with an ergonomic shape that is easy and comfortable to hold, and are fabricated in flexible plastic that is very resistant and can be carried in a sports bag.

< Form and design   **Shape and ergonomics**   Surface graphics >

Ergonomics

Ergonomics refers to the science of designing packaging to fit or facilitate human interactions with a product during consumption of it, and to a lesser extent to make for better ease of handling of a product as it travels through the distribution chain. Ergonomic design results in a product that is comfortable to use and that is unlikely to give rise to any cause of accident, injury or discomfort, such as the occurrence of repetitive strain injury, for instance.

Ergonomics therefore relates to how people interact with physical objects and seeks to improve the design of products in order to make such interactions more comfortable and to optimise both health and productivity.

In terms of packaging, designers frequently apply ergonomic principles in order to produce a more harmonious interaction between products and the human body. The presence of handles die-cut out of cartons of 12-packs of beer makes them much easier to hold; and washing detergents that have moulded hand grips with grooves for the user's fingers provides another good example of how ergonomics may be put to good use in packaging design.

L'Oréal

Freedom Of Creation created this striking limited-edition packaging for the launch of cosmetic producer L'Oréal's Gold Future eye reviver cream (below). The packaging is intriguing and expresses the preciousness of the product, which contains Micro-Active Gold. The organic spherical envelope, made with flexible nylon and 3D printing, was inspired by the fluidity of the cream, and the package is unwrapped in a soft, sensual, spiral movement that is also ergonomic.

Lofoten

Strømme Throndsen Design created this packaging for Norwegian bottled water brand, Lofoten (right). The design has a high-aspect ratio due to the long thin bottle design that differentiates the product from its lower-aspect ratio competitors. The minimalist bottles have a distinctive, angled blue cap and the bottles have the brand name moulded into them near the base. The bottle's shape invites users to actively explore it.

Vodka concept bottle

This Vodka bottle (left) represents a concept design created by the Russian designer Dzmitry Samal of Samal Design. It is a prime example of simplicity in packaging design as the packaging and form are one; they tell the same story and obviate the need for a label or explanation. In this concept, the brand is formed from the shape of the bottle, that appears as a mound of ice cubes made from crystal glass. 'The aim was to create an outstanding bottle which would be simple, characteristic and modern at the same time, and that would reflect the main quality of the vodka – its freshness,' says Samal.

< Form and design   **Shape and ergonomics**   Surface graphics >

Developing unique shapes
Some brands are so well known that they are recognisable even when you cannot see the labelling and overt brand communication. Here are four famous alcoholic beverage brands, photographed to highlight their shape and with their labels blocked out. Can you tell which brands are represented? This example is designed to help you think about the question of what makes a shape memorable, identifiable and distinctive. Developing a unique shape for a product can help to distinguish it from its competitors, can aid product recall in a retail environment and may also help to generate sales.

< Form and design   **Shape and ergonomics**   Surface graphics >

The big reveal! Here are the four bottles shown on the previous spread, but with their labels and brand information visible. Notice how their graphics support and enhance the brand value of each product, both through what they say and the visual impression that they convey. Observe how the bottles also contain sector cues. The brandy bottle (far left), has a curved shape that is typically associated with brandy bottles, and is also used by competing brandy brands. Copycat or 'me-too' brands often mimic or replicate the shape and/or colours of the brand leader, in the hope that consumers who are not paying attention when shopping may accidentally purchase their product by mistake instead.

< Shape and ergonomics   **Surface graphics**   Print finishing and materials >

Surface graphics

The following pages will look at how typography, illustration and photography are used on packaging designs to convey a message or a story once the USP has been determined.

Choosing an approach

Before a packaging approach can be decided upon, the design team and client need to decide which particular attribute of the product is to be especially presented and promoted. The USP of the product will normally be included within the design brief. However, this may be amended following research into how a brand is perceived by the market or what the market requirements are. There are many ways of telling the same story, for example through the use of words, images or a combination of both. The initial discussion and research will be focused around the overall approach, but as an exercise it is often useful to explore all possible routes. What would a piece of packaging look like if it were to be typographic only? How would the message be conveyed using photography or illustration?

Photography and illustration

Each of these routes has its own advantages. Typography is essentially descriptive; that is, you can easily explain to someone what the product is, or what its core values are. Photography is often used in an aspirational way, to convey a sense of ambition, or to show the detail and quality of a product. Meanwhile, illustration can allow the unimaginable to be imagined. In reality, one or more of these approaches is normally employed in a design scheme, and the boundaries between these disciplines can often be blurred or crossed.

Typography is often treated as image, being manipulated and altered to create graphic effect. Illustration and photography can also merge; overt manipulation can be used to make the real (a photograph, for instance) appear hyperreal or fantastical in its outcome.

West Elm

These shopping bags were created by Hatch Design for the furniture and home design products retailer West Elm and was one of several components designed to expand upon the new visual story developed. The bags feature silhouettes of home furnishing products, such as chairs and vases, reversed out of a neutral background colour together with the store name.

'Elegance is the simplicity found at the far side of complexity. An elegant solution is one in which the optimal outcome is achieved with the minimal expenditure of effort and expense.'

Matthew E May

Askul

This packaging for Japanese mail-order company Askul, by Stockholm Design Lab, shows a sense of playfulness in the structure of the design. Strong visual elements are used as icons, to enable instant identification of the product type. The copier paper (shown right and below), uses a series of strong, deconstructed graphic symbols, indicative of the product's intended use. The power of the brand is built up through the repetition of both the design elements and style, but also through the use of variation, as can be seen in the garbage bag packages (above). Here, the rigid structure of ranged-left typography literally 'falls' into a playful expression of the product's use.

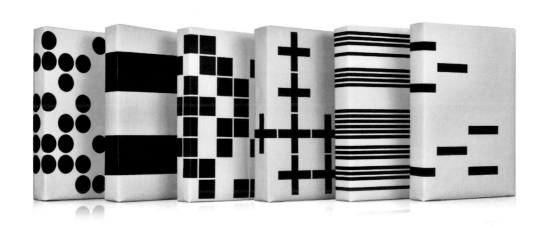

< Shape and ergonomics   **Surface graphics**   Print finishing and materials >

Photography

Photography fulfils many communication functions as part of packaging design; from the basic role of providing information, such as showing what a product looks like or how it can be used, to being much more sophisticated and conveying feelings that help to create the visual brand identity. Photography can make packaging more appealing to consumers through the use of glossy, four-colour printing that enables products to fight for attention in the retail environment.

Emotions or still life

Photography can communicate with consumers in different ways. It can provide hard-and-fast general information by simply showing the product; or it can suggest ideas and emotions that may help to engender a certain feeling towards a brand by expressing emotions or nuances. It can also be educative by demonstrating different product uses, such as by providing food product serving suggestions. Manufacturers show images of their products on packaging to help differentiate them from competing products or to highlight special features. Food manufacturers often use photography to show the freshness and quality of their product and to show how delicious it is.

A photograph can be very structured as the lighting, composition, arrangement, colouration and many other factors can be directly controlled. The aim of the images needs to be clear when commissioning a photographer and to ensure that they have sufficient experience to deliver the required results. Some photographers specialise in studio product shots, while others are known for their ability to create and represent different moods and emotions.

Photography may focus on providing stimuli to users that will be interpreted in a certain way based on their emotional experience, rather than merely denoting the product itself. Sometimes, products aren't shown at all.

Photographic considerations

A photograph can encapsulate brand characteristics and project them to the consumer using the tools of rhetoric (*logos* or logical proof, *pathos* or emotional persuasion, *ethos* or brand personality). This is particularly true when it may be hard for a consumer to differentiate between similar products. For example, the Superdrug depilation products on the facing page use a tastefully shot black-and-white image of a female model to create an emotional link to the product. Photography enables manufacturers to show consumers what a product will do or what it is like without the user actually needing to open the physical packaging.

Cropping

The final product of a photo shoot is a photo, but the creative use of photography does not end there. The way that a photo is cropped can dramatically alter the message that it delivers. Cropping directs the viewer to focus on what is important and removes or restricts what is not. Positioning the main element within the frame can make an image more or less dynamic and interesting. A symmetrical frame appears relatively static; an offset frame is more dynamic. Photographers and designers use tools like the rule of thirds and the rule of odds (illustrated below) to create arresting designs.

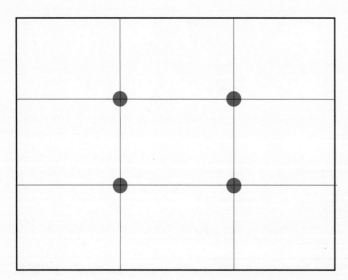

The rule of thirds: this divides a frame into nine sections and creates a dynamic hot spot for the placement of elements where the points cross.

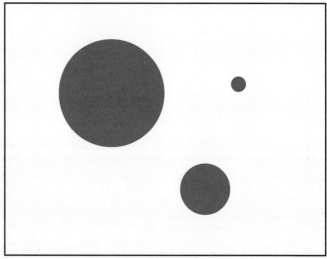

The rule of odds: this actually refers to using an *even* number of objects to frame, or support, the key element within the image.

'We have focused on the beautiful natural body, using high-contrast black-and-white photography that has a sheen effect, emphasising the smooth skin of the model and evoking the emotion of someone being at one and relaxed with the whole situation.'

Kasia Rust – creative director, burst*

Superdrug – female depilatory products

The female depilatory products pictured here were packaged by burst* for UK retail chemist Superdrug. The packaging uses photography as part of the range segmentation and to differentiate each product, while at the same time unifying them within the same line (the photograph shown on the left formed part of the shoot from which the product shots were extracted). Neil Mackenzie Matthews's photography is stylish and intimates the well being and graceful results that may be gained from use of the products. This is achieved through the use of focused light that plays on the smooth skin of the model. The photographic style aims to both inspire and empower the consumer.

EYEBROW SHAPERS
Long lasting hair removal in minutes
4 sleeves, each with 14 assorted
pre-cut strips to create
perfectly shaped eyebrows.

SENSITIVE
WAX STRIPS
For legs and body
Long-lasting hair removal.
10 double-sided wax strips with a
delicate lavender fragrance.
4 moisturising finishing wipes
with wheat germ oil.

FACE & BIKINI
WAX STRIPS
Long lasting hair removal.
10 double-sided wax strips with
a delicate lavender fragrance.
2 moisturising finishing wipes
with wheat germ oil.

3 MINUTE FORMULA
HAIR REMOVAL CREAM
For legs and body
With vitamin E for
beautifully smooth skin.
Dermatologically tested.

Style

A designer can take a photograph and style it in different ways to give it various qualities: reportage, Lomo, over-saturation, full colour, grayscale, archive or hyperreality, for instance. With film cameras, this would have been achieved using different photographic techniques, but with digital photography, this is more often performed on computers at the post-production stage.

The range of effects that are possible and the stylistic choices available will ultimately provide you with further potential to take ownership of a particular photographic style and make an image work in the way that you really desire. The images below and on the facing page show some of the different post-production styles that a photograph can be given, which can change both its feel and appearance. A photo can thus be styled to appeal to different emotions by revealing or concealing detail. The use of colour, for instance, generally results in a warmer feeling than does the use of black and white, and colour adjustments can make even more dramatic interventions.

The packaging for Dyson vacuum cleaners uses cut ways to show the product from the side, while consumer electronics firm Apple shoots its products straight on. Each company consistently uses a particular style, which through familiarity gained by repeated exposure, helps consumers to readily identify products and to distinguish them from others as they become accustomed to seeing them presented in a certain way. This familiarity crystallises into consumers actively seeking out a product's packaging when buying products.

Contrast

Contrast within photography refers to the juxtaposition of light and dark areas within an image. Contrast can add drama to an image due to this juxtaposition. Some camera lenses offer more contrast and allow for more subtle gradations of tone.

Focus

Each photo has a depth of field, which is the zone of sharpest focus. A photographer can alter the depth of field so that more or less of the subject matter is either in or out of focus. A narrow depth of field maintains a sharp focus on just one part of the subject and is a way of eliminating background visual noise. Using a narrow depth of field forces the viewer to look at the subject and disregard the background so that they only focus on the story that you are trying to tell.

Perspective

You should not assume that you always need to look at things in the same way. Simply changing perspective can yield interesting and positive results. Using photography provides the opportunity to explore a product and how it is approached and represented.

Depth of field: within photographic images, the depth of field (above) can be controlled, essentially altering the amount of the image that is in focus. This allows an emphasis to be placed on a particular portion of the image.

Photographic styles: there are a wealth of photographic styles, ranging from reportage, documentary and still life, and a range of values that can be altered, including contrast and brightness. This image (above) was shot in a Lomoesque style, where colours are muted and the edges of the frame become darker.

Nougat

Andy Vella created the packaging (above) for bodycare products for
UK brand, Nougat. Vella says, 'the designs were created to replace
the frumpy packaging previously designed and responded to a brief
specifying the need for the products to appeal to female buyers'.
The designs feature boxes made from thick translucent paper printed
with subtle floral designs which delicately cross the boundary between
illustration and photography to compelling effect. The products sold in
high-end London shops, such as Liberty's, Selfridges and Harrods.

Voyeur

New York based design agency Little Fury created the packaging below
for lingerie brand Voyeur. The packaging brought a naughty attitude to
everyday lingerie through a strong identity and intimate photography.
For instance, a bra is packaged in a pull-top can that says 'bra' on the
front; while body oil is packaged in an oil can that is labelled 'body oil'.

< Shape and ergonomics   **Surface graphics**   Print finishing and materials >

Tesco insect repellent

This packaging design for a range of insect repellent products was created by R Design for UK retailer, Tesco. It features a humorous illustration that depicts a dying fly circling to the ground, presumably following use of the product, the purpose of which is instantly communicated to the user. Note how the bold red and yellow colours deployed act to warn consumers that the contents may be harmful.

Illustration

The Industrial Revolution (c1760–1850) fundamentally changed the way in which products were manufactured and subsequently sold. Combined with the advent of lithographic printing, the Industrial Revolution gave rise to the practice of commercial art and, later, graphic design. For the first time, high-quality printing was both widely available and affordable, and an increase in manufacturing fuelled consumer thirst for ever more products. As more products gradually became available commercially, the need for differentiation between one brand and another also therefore greatly increased.

Historically, products with a physical form that are not inherently interesting or self-explanatory (such as washing powder, for example), have made great use of illustration to convey ideas about their characteristics. Illustration provides an invaluable 'public face' for products, and is a technique that is able to both decorate (make desirable) and inform, in a way that other disciplines, such as photography, cannot.

The simplicity of illustration enables designers to readily explain a product or convey an idea or concept, thereby communicating its values and its uses. Illustration can also be realistic and accurately portray what a product is essentially like; or alternately, it can be abstract and so convey an impression of a specific sensation that a product may incite, for instance. The creative freedom offered by illustration enables a designer to communicate the intrinsic values associated with a product rather than specific information about its constituent ingredients or elements. In the case of washing powder, to return to our example, these values may be concerned with the product's primary functions, that is to produce cleanness and freshness; or with its price point, that is, whether it is a luxury or economy product. Neither of these factors have anything to do with the product contained within the packaging, in terms of what it actually is.

Illustration thus allows for the isolated focus of a core proposition. It is safe to assume that all washing powders generally clean clothes, and that all leave the clothes smelling fresh; but some may choose to focus on the product's environmental credentials, while others may instead market themselves on value. Most products, be they large or small, complex or simple, have more than one facet or prime characteristic that they could choose to market themselves on. However, the principal aim of packaging design is to clearly and succinctly tell a simple story that the consumer can understand and relate to immediately. The examples that we will encounter over the following pages are testament to the clarity of thought that illustration can bring to packaging design.

Different 'hands'

Illustrators have their own unique style or 'hands', so sourcing an illustrator for a job usually requires obtaining samples of the work, or 'book', of several different people in order to find a style that most fits with what you aim to do or achieve with a given design. It is also important to familiarise yourself with some basic illustration techniques, such as woodcut, engraving and print-making, to be better able to brief and direct a commissioned illustrator, as each technique invariably produces a different 'feel'.

Personification

Once a particular illustration or style has been decided on, the opportunity exists to scale out the design to other products within the same brand or category. The characterisation can be used over multiple items or lines to create a sense of continuity and ownership for the brand. Many products are difficult to differentiate from those of their competitors, but by personifying them through branded packaging and the use of a brand personality, the product has much more of a chance of becoming widely recognised.

In the example below, the range of nappies shown may become known as the brand with the elephant on, thus positing a much stronger brand proposition than does 'Superdrug nappies'. The use of animal images on the baby-care range of Superdrug products creates a warm and soft brand image that results in a positive sensation and association with them. Effectively, the branded products personify those same feelings that people exhibit towards babies, for whom the products are designed.

Rocombe Farm

Reach's rebrand for a premium ice-cream produced by Rocombe Farm features the use of illustrations (above). Market research showed that consumers expressed a preference for the product to display a feel of 'Britishness' and a sense of eccentricity. This was captured by dressing each flavour in illustrated outfits that mimic quality, tailored clothes that convey the sophistication of the organic product, with each flavour presented as a clothing label.

Superdrug – baby range

The packaging shown here forms part of the baby range created by burst* for UK retail chemist Superdrug and features illustrations by Sophie Mockford (below). A bold, graphic animal theme reminiscent of children's books was designed to engage both mother and child. The iconic animal images identify the products on the shelf and help people to remember which product to buy – the red elephant nappies, for example. Each package identifies the baby age that the nappies are suitable for in large bold type to make product selection simpler. The design scheme opts for simplicity thereby differentiating it from the chaotic graphic mess that tends to dominate the nappy sector.

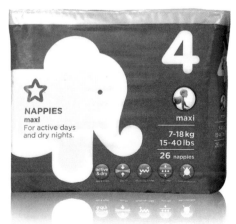

Green & Spring

Pearlfisher created this packaging for hand-made beauty brand Green & Spring featuring graphics inspired by the English countryside, which reinforce that the products contain 100 per cent natural botanical materials with all herbs, flowers and plants used native to the UK. Each bird represents a product within the three ranges with additional segmentation provided by different colour palettes directly linked to the emotions associated with them.

Wine of Design

The innovative and non-traditional packaging approach developed by 3 Deep Design for Wine of Design 2009 and pictured here gave a new twist to wine packaging. The labels make extensive use of illustration to create energetic designs that capture the imagination and stand out from the staid traditional labels that the product will be in competition with on the shelf.

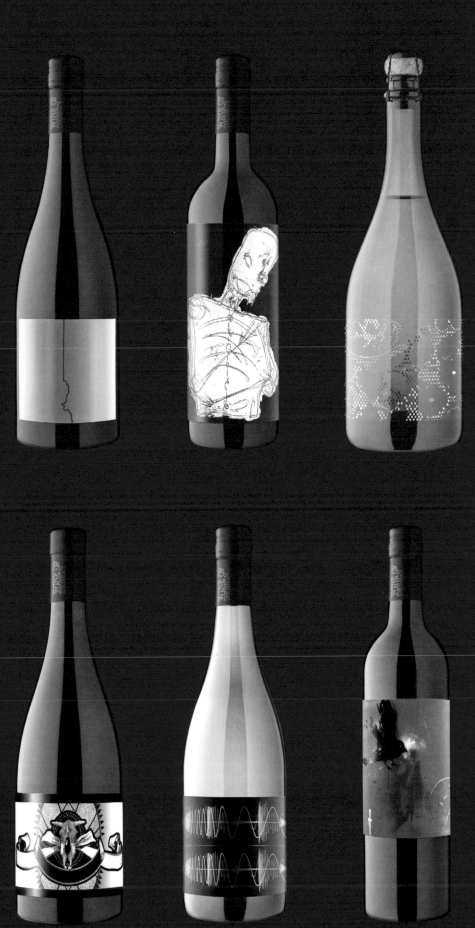

< Shape and ergonomics   **Surface graphics**   Print finishing and materials >

Selfridges

A bold new brand identity was created by R Design for prestigious UK retailer, Selfridges (below). Selfridges had taken the radical step of transforming its traditional brand identity from that of purveyor of high-quality goods to modern, forward-looking and fashionable retailer. The London store's interior changed to reflect this, and R Design's packaging was created with the same bold attitude. The combination of black background and coloured text creates a distinctive and unique brand identity for Selfridges's own label products, and has dramatic on-shelf impact. The packaging was quick to get noticed and a string of design awards followed.

Bonita

Z3 Design created the packaging pictured (above) for computer-generated effects software company Bonita. The packaging creates slick sequencing to open and access the product, and its instruction booklet reinforces the operational qualities of the software contained within it.

'This really is the new black.'

R Design

Typography

Typography is an inherent part of packaging design and in the role that packaging has to play in communicating information about the product to the consumer, such as the name of the product, its manufacturer, date of manufacture, ingredients and safety information. The ease and clarity with which text communicates is an important factor in the success of the packaging in connecting with a consumer or user. Poor communication will lead to frustration and consumers moving onto another product.

The breadth, depth and flexibility of typography means that it is an integral part of establishing a brand identity and a determinant factor in the ability of packaging to successfully communicate. The plethora of typefaces and styles gives designers an incredible palette with which to work from and produce creative ideas; given that the personality characteristics of typefaces can transfer directly to the product.

Typeface personality

Type not only communicates by what it says but by *how* it says it. Different typefaces and typeface styles add their own peculiar elements to the communication that can lead the reader to interpret it in different ways. Some types appear stern and conservative, while others are more relaxed and even jovial. Designers can select or create typefaces that have the desired attributes and characteristics of the brand as a way to reinforce the brand message. As many products are essentially very similar, the battle for sales tends to be conducted by the perceived personalities or attributes of a product, which are often established in the packaging. The use of typeface personality is an essential part of establishing the perceived characteristics of a brand personality.

Scale

Typefaces can be used at different scales or point sizes. Size not only affects how readable a piece of text is but also allows text to work as a graphic element in its own right. Designers talk of text colour when they are referring to how text fills and 'colours' a particular space; and a block of text colour will relate to and interact with other aspects of the design's colour, such as images and white space. Type size is also one of the means used to establish a hierarchy of information, such as by drawing attention to the brand name or the product name, or to other important information.

Agrovim

Greek design agency Mouse created the packaging pictured (right) for a premium olive oil by Agrovim. It features typography set in different point sizes to highlight the premium quality of the product and to effect visual differentiation. The design scheme represents a deliberate move away from clichéd olive oil packaging imagery, and the use of a realistic-looking drop of oil keeps the design grounded.

Serious *Happy*
Modern TECHNO
Old fashioned
Western
Informal 𝔊𝔬𝔱𝔥𝔦𝔠

Different typefaces: each has a very different look, feel and 'personality' that designers can use to help position a brand within a consumer's mind (above).

< Shape and ergonomics   **Surface graphics**   Print finishing and materials >

Oy! - organic young

The Oy! organic young range of cosmetic products for teenagers features packaging created by burst* for Green People (above), along with the prominent use of typography and illustrations by Sophie Mockford. The typographic style, icons and bold use of colour are designed to communicate directly to teenagers and to respond to their concerns about, and awareness of, environmental issues.

Bitter Sisters

Shane Cranford created the bottle and label designs for cocktail mixers brand Bitter Sisters, shown below. They feature a range of typographic scales and various visual cues, while the typography draws on historical associations to health tonics – a reference that is reinforced by the brown bottle, traditionally used for medicines and tonics.

Korott Laboratories

These toothpaste tubes created by Lavernia & Cienfuegos for Korott Laboratories feature typography to differentiate the brand from other products and efficiently communicate the specialist nature of the dental care range (right). The typographic solution is very functional and can be read easily. The overlapping of the letters and their transparencies provide graphic richness to personalise the range and indicate the quality of the products.

Orrefors

Pictured below is packaging created by Neumeister for Swedish custom glassware manufacturer Orrefors. Marketed under the 'Love is Divine' theme, designer Erika Lagerbielke's concept is represented by subtle and understated surface graphics that show the glassware lit against a black background.

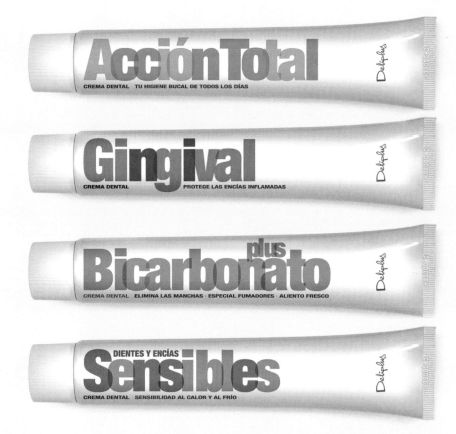

< Surface graphics   **Print finishing and materials**   Front and back of pack >

Print finishing and materials
Various print finishing methods and materials are available by which designers can add the final touches to a packaging design, which can help to both transform it into something very special and add value to a brand.

The surface graphics created as part of packaging design can be imparted to the packaging in many ways other than printing them on the packaging substrate. These include burning, screen-printing (serigraphy), embossing and foil blocking, amongst others. The use of different finishing techniques to apply visual elements onto a substrate can help to further differentiate a brand.

As the graphics are applied separately to the surface of the packaging, the product manufacturer maintains a degree of flexibility in that they can choose to change the packaging's visual appearance without interfering with its production, to a certain extent – perhaps to rebrand, update or include a promotion. The actual production process does not have to be retooled. Some main choices for consideration are explored in detail below.

Burning
An image can be burned into a wooden substrate using a heated steel dye or brand. This is a medium-volume method that adds a touch of elegance to a product. Think of camembert cheese boxes, boxes of wine and wine corks, for example.

Shrink-film labels
A high-volume method that shrink-wraps film labels around a container with an uneven contour to provide a continuous surface for an image. Think of bottles of chilli sauce or yoghurt drinks, for example.

Film labels
A high-volume method that wraps film labels around a bottle container to provide a continuous surface for an image, such as for bottled water.

Adhesive labels
A high-volume method whereby paper or plastic labels are stuck onto the front and back surfaces of a container, as with jam jars, for example.

Paper wraparound labels
A high-volume method that wraps paper labels around a cylindrical container to provide a continuous surface for an image. Think of tuna cans as an example.

Direct offset printing
A high-volume method whereby an image is directly printed onto the container, such as with aluminium drinks cans.

Hand painting
A low-volume method whereby a design is painted by hand on to each container to add a unique element.

Embossing
A low-volume method that involves embossing a design into a metal, paper or board substrate that leaves an attractive, tactile finish.

Foil blocking
A low-volume method that involves a design being foil-blocked onto a paper or board substrate in order to add an attractive detail.

Deboss
A low-volume method that involves creating a design that is then debossed into a metal, paper or board substrate leaving an attractive and tactile sunken finish.

Varnish
A high-volume method that applies a protective coating to a substrate that may also add a visual finish, such as shine or matt.

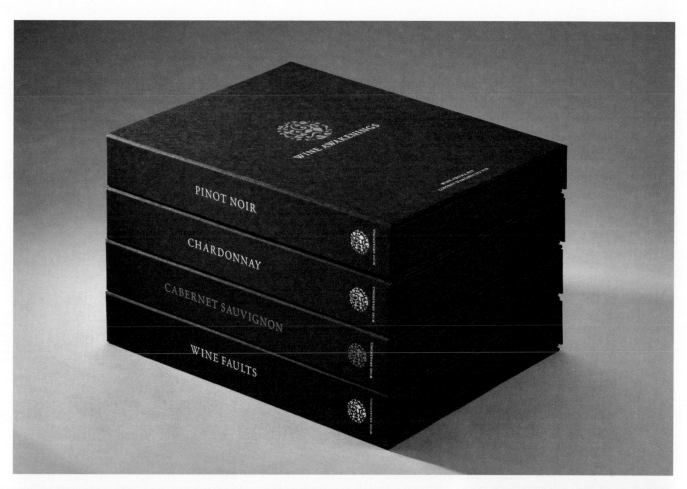

Wine Awakenings

Mookai Communications, Canada, created this packaging for Wine Awakenings for a wine aroma kit that helps sommeliers and wine enthusiasts to identify the various flavour notes contained in different wines. The nature of the product is exclusive and sophisticated, qualities which were transmitted by the new packaging design. 'The Wine Aroma Kits were repackaged with matte black paper and the logos were foil stamped in colours representing the different wine varieties. Inside the kit are the aroma vials, an informative brochure and a set of illustrated scent cards,' explains Mookai.

< Surface graphics   **Print finishing and materials**   Front and back of pack >

Choosing materials

The first consideration that needs to be made when selecting packaging materials concerns their ability to successfully contain the product. A packaged form can make a great contribution to the narrative and intent that a brand seeks to establish. The second packaging consideration is therefore the different shapes that can be created to build and develop a brand narrative. Finally, a designer needs to consider the surface graphics that will adorn the packaging solution and present the brand to the target market. These three elements may be decided upon separately, consecutively or may emerge organically as a design idea is worked up. The materials guide on this page highlights some basic considerations about the appropriate use of materials and looks at their particular strengths, weaknesses, costs and the ease with which surface graphics can be applied to them.

Steel

Solid, strong container for liquids and foods, high protection, takes printed paper labels and recyclable; but heavy in weight and with limited shaping ability.

Aluminium

Strong container for liquids, high protection, printable and recyclable; but involves energy-intensive production and has limited shaping ability.

PVC or LDPE (low-density polyethylene) films

Lightweight, transparent and low cost; but may be easy to tear and is difficult to print and recycle. Generally used to package food.

Wood

The original packaging material, wood is used to crate large items for shipping and is also used for creating presentation boxes, as for wine. It can be heat-branded with graphics and readily takes paper labels.

LDPE

Strong film, lightweight, pliable, mouldable, and printable. Used for plastic bags, trays, general purpose containers and food storage. LDPE is recyclable but it is also difficult to separate.

Paper bag

These are lightweight, low cost and easy to print and recycle; but they are also easy to tear and have limited shape capability.

Polypropylene

A thermoplastic polymer that is resistant to fatigue. Used for plastic living hinges, such as flip-top bottles, food containers that do not melt during industrial hot-filling processes and plastic disposable bottles.

Plastic bag

Lightweight, low cost and easy to print; but easy to tear (depending upon film thickness) and with limited shape capability. Falling out of favour due to environmental impact and consumers' failure to recycle.

Paper

Wraps items of any shape, is lightweight with excellent print surface, is low cost, recyclable; but easy to tear and lacks strength.

Tetra Pak

Strong container for liquids, high protection, lightweight and with an excellent print surface; but is more difficult to recycle.

Cardboard

Strong, high protection, excellent print surface, lightweight, low cost and recyclable; but with limited shape production.

Glass

Strong container for liquids, easy to mould, high protection, takes shrink-wrap labels, recyclable; but energy-intensive production, limited printing ability, harmful if broken.

HDPE (high-density polyethylene)

Strong, robust container for liquids such as detergents, is lightweight, mouldable, takes paper labels and is recyclable. Typically used for detergents, bottles and plastic bags.

Shrink-wrap or shrink film

Polyolefin or PVC film that can be heat shrunk around any shape, is lightweight and low cost; but difficult to recycle or print, and easy to tear.

Haçienda

Andy Vella created this unique packaging for a deluxe foil-blocked limited edition of *The Haçienda: How Not to Run a Club* by Peter Hook, produced by the bespoke publishing house Foruli. The iconic design features a Canadian maple hand-printed box containing pieces of mounted granite bar and floor from the original Haçienda club in Manchester, UK; it also comprises a fully hand-sewn, hand-bound and hand-printed book contained in a laser-engraved, glow-edge perspex case, resulting in a visually stunning piece of original artwork as packaging design.

< Surface graphics   **Print finishing and materials**   Front and back of pack >

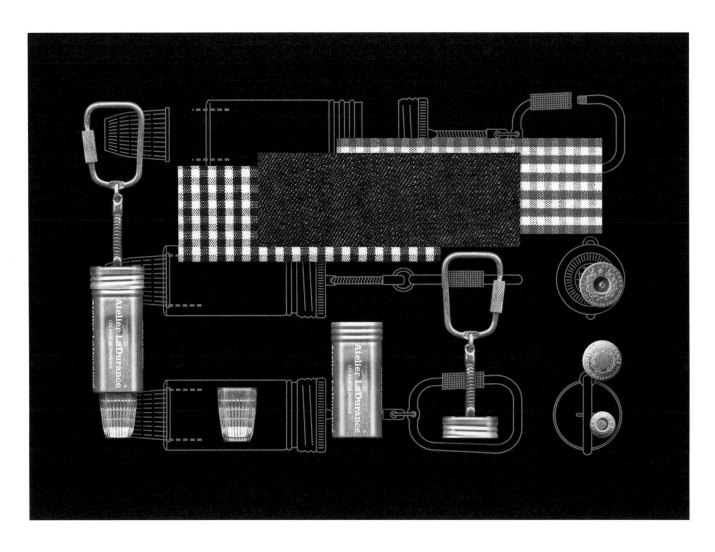

Atelier LaDurance

Dutch designer Boy Bastiaens created the branded packaging here for Atelier LaDurance. Featuring aspects of denim manufacture, the keyring repair kit capsule (top left) is the brand's major identifier and contains a thimble, two buttons, a piece of lining and a piece of denim in the quality of the purchased garment. The promotional Japanese denim packaging (bottom left) constitutes a fine bamboo mat wrapped around a folded pair of jeans that bears an enlarged screen-print of the jean's quality tag. The leather belt packaging (bottom right) is a sheet of white machine-coated board folded around the belt and attached with two brass-split pins.

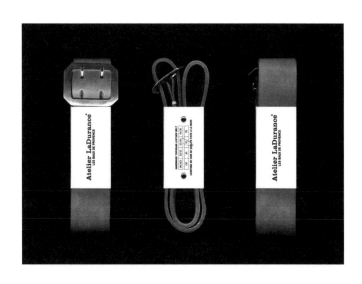

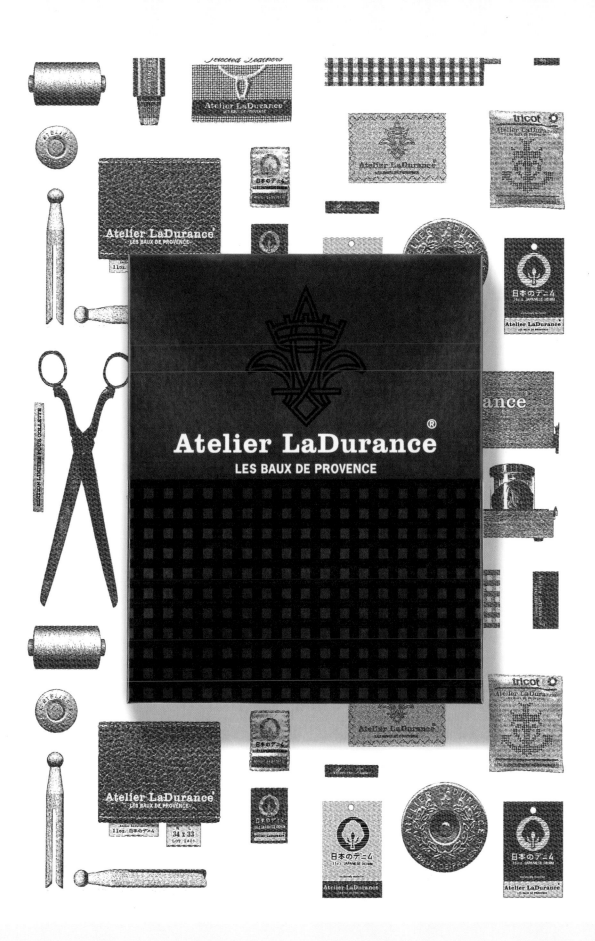

This gift box (above) for Atelier LaDurance's cashmere pullovers features a Vichy check pattern and fleur-de-lis design printed with UV spot varnish, shown against Atelier LaDurance wrapping paper. It features a repeating pattern of scraperboard images of its different branding items on 22-gram Italian sulphite paper.

< Surface graphics   **Print finishing and materials**   Front and back of pack >

Foster 40

The book *Foster 40* features the work and themes of renowned British architect Sir Norman Foster, and was created to celebrate the 40th anniversary of his practice (below, and right). The book by Thomas Manss & Company comes in two hinged hardback volumes contained within a hinged slipcase presentation box. The unusual product configuration creates a more interesting object to interact with that gives the reader a tangible experience of the projects.

Silver Island

Many packaging designs rely on translating the brand to the physical form. This detailing determines whether or not the final package will be a success. Shown below is a brand created by Prague-based Creasence design. The logo is translated into a physical form through the use of a silver foil (right), adding a tactile element to the final design.

David Bromley

Created by 3 Deep Design for work by artist David Bromley, this special edition three-book set was contained in a special satchel outer, which acts as a metaphor for the content of the work that includes a volume about children, providing a very physical interaction experience.

< Surface graphics   **Print finishing and materials**   Front and back of pack >

Bringing it all together

The previous spreads have looked separately at materials, photography, illustration and typography as distinct design elements. Ultimately, all of these elements are combined in the final resolve of a project in order to create the final branded product. While working on optimising each individual element, a designer also needs to consider them simultaneously so that they come together coherently and harmoniously.

From the attitude or tone of the promotional photography through to the typographic detailing and the subtlety of the illustration style, a balance needs to be struck so that all the elements employed combine to work successfully together. For marketing purposes, it is usual to create a 'hero' image, that is, a single image that encapsulates the essence of the brand, as shown below.

BUTA'I

This branding by Dan Alexander & Co demonstrates how all the elements have been brought together into a single package. The final packaging features embossing and foiling; typography, illustration and surface-printing details, like the use of silver foil, which all combine to create the final packaged brand.

'Hero' photography used for both press relations and in-store merchandising.

Support material, or 'collateral', showing considerations of material and form.

Armormount

G Workshop Design created this packaging redesign for Armormount mount systems with a small budget and a brief that stipulated the need to continue using the existing product images. The photography allows the product to play the protagonist through the boldness of its form, giving immediacy to the packaging and using colour as a counterpoint to characterise the main product lines.

< Print finishing and materials   Front and back of pack   Case study >

Front and back of pack

There has been a recent shift in emphasis with regard to the information that manufacturers communicate to consumers – from the back to the front of pack (FOP). This has occurred as a direct response to the type of information that people now actively seek out. People are more conscious about their health and want to eat more healthily; they are also increasingly concerned about how products are made and the nature of their ingredients and materials. Manufacturers have responded to such consumer concerns by repositioning such information where it can be most easily seen – onto the front label.

Social concerns

Society undergoes periodic cultural shifts in terms of what it deems most important and product manufacturers have to cater to such changes accordingly. People are increasingly concerned about their impact on the environment and the conditions under which the goods that they purchase have been produced. The migration of product information from the back of a packet to the front reflects such changes, which aims to make decision-making more informed and so easier. An increasing percentage of label space is also given over to providing useful product information to consumers rather than to merely promoting a brand message.

In the UK, use of the Soil Association symbol endorses the sustainable production practices of the manufacturer, thereby adding to product credibility.

Many manufacturers adopt a system to specify the calorific, fat and salt content of foods. This example uses milestones, which aims to simplify this information.

A global cultural shift has taken place, which has placed greater emphasis on how things are produced. Food products must now be organic, low fat, locally produced or 100 per cent natural too, and such characteristics qualify the brand's position before the consumer; these qualities can all serve as suffixes for yoghurt, for instance.

Creative thinking

There is an axiom that packaging has to present important information on the front of the pack while secondary information is presented on the reverse. This distinction means that a packaging design tends to break down into performing two distinct tasks, where the front of pack tells us the high level product message such as what it is and what it stands for, while the reverse carries the detailed product information such as what it is made from, where it came from or how to use it. These conventions can be broken or done away with through the use of creative thinking to present consumers with something unexpected that catches the eye and differentiates a product.

Icons and symbols

The surface graphics on packaging are often complemented by visual information that is included in order to meet statutory requirements or to provide generic useful information. This is particularly the case for food, pharmaceutical, cosmetic or degradable products, those that present a variety of hazards or those that have particular recycling requirements.

Packaging designers have to accommodate a range of obligatory communications, such as information about weights and measures, country of origin, nutrition and ingredients information, and health warnings, much of which can be easily communicated via various symbol systems that have been developed for such an end. In addition, most manufactured products have to show their country of manufacture. Many labeling symbols are nationally or internationally standardized, such as recycling symbols, the resin identification codes and the Green Dot. Bar codes, Universal Product Codes and RFID labels are also common to allow automated information management in logistics and retailing.

Back Label Wines

Pictured above are bottles created by Australia's Voice for Back Label, a value wine brand that features a creative label concept. Back Label competes in the cleanskin wine segment, which is where wineries get rid of excess wine stocks without discounting their main brands. The design solution features a single-colour screen-printed label with reversed-out lettering printed in reverse to appear backwards on the front label. This lettering appears correctly when viewed from the back of the bottle whereby it is magnified by the glass.

Additional elements

Packaging, particularly for fast-moving consumer goods (FMCGs), often has to accommodate additional temporary design elements that inform consumers about special promotions or price discounts. These often take the form of roundels, flashes and offers.

The roundel

A roundel is a circular device that mimics a stamp or seal (as shown above). Roundels are not part of the main design and their nature implies that they have been added afterwards, principally as an endorsement of quality. Many logos, such as those providing organic endorsement, for example, often take this form. Roundels aim to give an impression of quality, but the claim has to be believable. The inclusion of such design elements may require a slight reorganisation of the main brand design in order to accommodate them.

Some roundels assume a more permanent presence than others. For example, information elements that were once communicated on the reverse of a pack now often appear as symbols on the front, such as nutritional information or the Soil Association logo, given that organic produce has increasingly become a mainstream selling point.

Flash

A flash is a stripe that is clearly separate from the overall packaging communication. A flash is similar to a belly band on a book or a ribbon on a present. It is an extra detail that is often printed with a *trompe l'oeil* drop shadow, which may be used to communicate such information as a new product size or weight.

Offers

Offers typically communicate when something extra is being given to the consumer over and above the normal product offering, such as the inclusion of 25 per cent more product for the same price. Offers are typically made using strategic numbers, that is those that people particularly respond to. Manufacturers will often give an extra percentage of the product free, such as 50 per cent extra, or will focus on the physical amount where the actual percentage would result in an inconvenient number, for example, by stating that the product is offered with 100ml extra free (rather than stating that there is an additional 13 per cent free). Key numbers are usually presented on a large scale as these can capture attention well; for example, '100ml' may involve the '100' being made larger than the 'ml', which will be rendered much smaller in relation to it.

Tie-ins

Brands seek to gain a temporary lift in market share through the use of tie-ins with films or other events, such as the FIFA World Cup, as consumers may be more pre-disposed to buy a product that has a link with an external event that they are especially interested in. In this way, public figures, personalities or characters that the general public are familiar with often appear seamlessly on branded packaging, be that Shrek, the Toy Story characters, or footballers such as Lionel Messi.

Walk Socks

Pictured left is the packaging created by Greek design agency Mouse for Walk Socks, a manufacturer of women's tights that feature humour to differentiate the packs in a market where they tend to look the same. The design features images that appear to be murder scene photographs in which only the legs of the victims can be seen, giving a good view of the tights that they're wearing. This Walk S(h)ocks idea targeted a rather mischievous consumer, with a well developed black sense of humour.

Roundels, tie-ins, offers and flashes

Here are several products that feature roundels, tie-ins, offers and flashes, which are routinely carried by a variety of branded packaging. Notice how the size of some of these devices dwarves the product logo and branding as the aim is to instantly grab consumer attention.

< Front and back of pack   **Case study**   Student exercise >

Case study
Gourmet Settings
Monnet Design

Design agency Monnet Design created the packaging featured in this case study for the retailer Costco. The packaging is for the Gourmet Settings range of cutlery products, which is presented in boxes with different numbers of pieces, and continues Gourmet Settings' tradition of clean, modern packaging. Updated with new colours, patterns, photography and printing techniques, Monnet's designs provide a new visual image for the products so that they stand out on the shelf and enable consumers to see the products more clearly, and that incorporate a new materials usage philosophy principally aimed at reducing the company's environmental impact.

Creating the structure of the boxes is typically the first step in the design process. These feature a viewing window that allows consumers to view all of the pieces of cutlery included in the set at a glance. The clean-and-simple design is coupled with straightforward copywriting to enable consumers to quickly identify all the product features. 'We have worked to make copy more didactic and easy to understand while maintaining a few moments of quirkiness and humour which give the brand its personality. The sparing use of copy and graphics is what gives the packaging its elegance,' says the designer.

Before a box goes into final production, there are several rounds of approval. Several design options are presented, often using different printing processes, such as foil stamping and matte and gloss varnishes. Mock-ups are made in China where the packaging is printed and assembled, and the president of Gourmet Settings and her marketing team help to decide which boxes will be then presented to store buyers. The final decision as to which boxes are chosen is often made by the store buyers directly.

'The brand character is not maintained through the consistent use of one colour, like many brands. The boxes are easily identified by their simplicity, their bold colours or patterns, their fun and informative copy, as well as the consistent use of Helvetica across all packaging,' explain Monnet Design.

Clever use of space enables the buyer to see the entire contents of the packaging at a glance (left). There is also a layering of information, with the logo and key facts in the foreground, the product in the mid-ground, and the use of a super graphic in the background. This creates a sense of space and order.

To streamline production, these four 20-piece boxes use a generic outer box design, with each one having its own coloured inner tray to differentiate it from the others when on the store shelf (left). The innovative box structures were created by Kerr+Company in collaboration with Gourmet Settings' own in-house industrial designer.

The 20-piece product from Easy Settings, (a sub-brand of Gourmet Settings) is packaged in a box that is part of a pilot project to reduce environmental impact by eliminating the use of PVC in its packaging and instead used 100 per cent recycled pulp paper trays (below). The pilot was successful and has since been put into full production.

Shown below are shipping boxes for small web orders that feature the GS logo. The playful tessellation of the logo, which wraps around the container, helps to create a strong brand positioning.

< Case study   Student exercise   Chapter 5 >

Student exercise

Type and image

Project set by Nigel Aono-Billson

Shown above are three accomplished packaging design projects, previously discussed on pages 151–158. One uses illustration as its main means of communication, one typography, and the other photography. All of these mediums are capable of conveying complex messages, but what are the advantages and disadvantages of each?

Can packaging design be art? Andy Warhol's Brillo Box almost certainly was. Packaging design often wins awards, like the range created for Selfridges in the UK by R Design (pictured here, middle left). This own-label range of packaging, from comestibles to household items, could be considered the epitome of stylish and artful design.

Brands such as Coca-Cola or Chanel are classic and are considered timeless, with their individual personalities established through their use of colour, shape/structure and distinctive typography. On the packaging itself, the physical or structural design has the power to do many things; it can create a product ethos, communicate a message, become an icon, stand for quality, be innovative or even command allegiance. But how can we get our message across to the consumer?

Student exercise

How to create a package with type and image

Through the usage of photography, illustration and typography, or a combination of these, packaging designers can create a design or range of designs that have shelf standout or extended shelf life in mind. Such design pieces should be in keeping with current or future market trends and should exude quality, inventiveness and style. A product with its own distinct character that is found on a massive scale is the humble chocolate bar. A visit to any supermarket will show the visual clamour that takes place between competing brands, all of which are desperate to be seen and chosen. These products, that offer a delicious experience, maybe with extras such as nuts, dried fruit or other flavours, need the addition of a personality.

1. Create

Packaging for a chocolate bar or range of chocolate bars. The design could express fun, humour, style, appeal and emotional communications. The message to the consumer must be artisanal, eclectic and handmade. The image or message could be formed from quirkiness, cultural references, historical references, a varied use of typestyles or typefaces, a distinctive illustration, or a specific photographic style.

The resulting design should have authenticity, be targeted, packaged and ultimately be aimed at an appropriate consumer group. The brand name or name style should provide a unique identity for the product, be memorable and easy to pronounce. Emphasis may be placed on quality, taste/flavour or the ingredients contained within the product – but the product should, above all, appear to the consumer to be utterly delicious.

You may also wish to consider national and international trends, markets and communities, as well as consumer groups, usage, relationships and gender. Also consider the retail outlets for final product distribution: for example, will it be branded or own label; sold in a supermarket, retail outlet, café or restaurant?

2. Consider:
- shape, form, size, weight, quantity and volume;
- look at similar products and brands;
- record any similarities and dissimilarities;
- note the uniqueness of colour ways and key colours used.

3. Explore
- Look at existing identities and brands.
- Consider the benefits of organic versus fair trade products.
- Compare high-quality and low-quality products.
- Study individual packaging structures and associated materials.
- Opening procedures, storage and wrapping.
- All the sensory associations and experiences that the product might offer.
- The product's history and origins.

Bibliography and further reading
Davis, M. (2009). *The Fundamentals of Branding*. AVA Publishing.

Gingko Press, (2008). *Simply Packaging*. Viction Design Workshop.

Grip Design, (2008). *1,000 Package Designs: A Complete Compilation of Creative Containers*. Rockport Publishers.

Milton, H. (1991). *Packaging Design: Smith and Milton (Issues in design)*. Design Council.

Olins, W. (2008). *Wally Olins: The Brand Handbook*. Thames & Hudson.

The future

The term 'future shock' describes a condition of distress and disorientation that is brought on by the inability to cope with rapid societal and technological change. It was first coined by the sociologist Alvin Toffler in his book of the same title in 1970, in which he described future shock as 'too much change in too short a period of time'.

Change can be gradual, incremental or evolutionary, or it can be rapid and dramatic. Either way, change is a constant, whether it comes in the form of adapting consumer perceptions or ethics or new technologies and communication possibilities.

Whatever changes happen now or in the future, brands will continue to need to communicate their qualities and advantages to potential consumers. The challenge for designers lies in being able to identify and embrace the current changes that are taking place in society and to present successful communication strategies that will work effectively with them.

< Introduction   **Key text**   Changing retail environments >

'Societies have always been shaped more by the nature of the media by which men communicate than by the content of the communication. The alphabet, for instance, is a technology that is absorbed by the very young child in a completely unconscious manner, by osmosis, so to speak. Words and the meaning of words predispose the child to think and act automatically in certain ways. The alphabet and print technology fostered and encouraged a fragmenting process of specialism and of detachment. Electric technology fosters and encourages unification and involvement. It is impossible to understand social and cultural changes without a knowledge of the workings of media.'

Marshall McLuhan, 1967

The Medium is the Massage

Marshall McLuhan

Packaging exists within an environment that helps to condition the way in which we see it; how a product is positioned in a store and how that store is decorated, for example, will influence our perception of it. Packaging also in turn helps to create the environment within which it exists; a wall containing only a single product, for instance, will exert a palpable physical and visual presence within a shop.

Packaging design ultimately seeks to go beyond the product to promote ideas that will appeal to consumers, such as of a beautiful, successful or healthy lifestyle, or by communicating concepts and characteristics that may be only distantly related to a product (or even not at all), such as saving the planet, for example.

The messages we receive from or perceive about packaging can condition us to behave in certain ways and make us believe that a product is more appealing than we might otherwise consider it to be. Do we essentially buy products for what they are or are consumers more interested in buying into their packaging, especially when making impulse purchases? Does the media shape society, as Marshall McLuhan suggests in his seminal book, *The Medium is the Massage*, a society within which media communication has become more important than the content?

The ability of packaging design to communicate specific brand messages is most challenged in the retail environment, where a product needs to be able to directly speak to (or shout at) the consumer; as well as to compete and create a space that physically 'contains' the consumer. Packaging designers therefore have to carefully consider the environmental aspects of the packaging's presentation so that the brand communication strategies can work at a larger scale than the product itself and be appropriately extrapolated or expanded upon.

What impact does an abundance of choice have on consumers? In *The Paradox of Choice: why more is less*, Barry Schwartz points out a fundamental paradox intrinsic to consumer society: that having choice is great, but having too much choice can become merely cumbersome. Whether buying fruit juice, jeans or cars, bitter regret may follow a purchase if and when something better becomes available on the market. Schwartz claims that an excess of choice can make us unhappy, so as consumers we should aim to limit the number of choices we make, even as the modern world designs to draw us into the realms of infinite choice.

< Key text   Changing retail environments   Environmental considerations >

Changing retail environments

The retail environments of the future will provide new challenges to packaging designers as they turn to embrace more information technology, including virtual retail, and as consumers require more precise product information. Packaging design will play an increasingly important role in helping retailers to meet their legal and corporate commitments to environmental sustainability.

Virtual packaging

The emergence of Internet or online sales has enabled many product manufacturers to make substantial savings to their distribution costs as they move away from traditional bricks-and-mortar retail outlets. Most product manufacturers now have virtual stores where people can order products directly for delivery to their homes or offices. The online distribution channel also gives vendors the opportunity to reach markets and consumers that they have traditionally been unable to reach solely through their store outlets. Certain product categories sell particularly well from virtual stores, such as music and books, as consumers can listen to songs and read extracts from books while online and therefore shop anywhere that they choose.

People will always desire to physically touch and try out products prior to purchase and so bricks-and-mortar stores will certainly continue to exist for the foreseeable future. Currently, most product sales continue to take place via retail outlets and online sales are largely viewed as an extension to traditional distribution channels. A traditional packaging philosophy and approach therefore still tends to dominate the market.

The most successful retailers are likely to be those that make the transition to selling through multiple channels, thereby providing consumers with all the buying options required in the contemporary market. Product packaging in this environment therefore needs to work equally well in both the online and retail milieux, as it would prove uneconomical to produce different packaging solutions for each. Creating packaging for products designed to generate sales for virtual stores presents packaging designers with additional challenges.

Virtual distribution

The existence of a virtual distribution channel does not mean that traditional brand packaging concepts are no longer valid; it rather suggests that they will need to be tweaked to respond to the new opportunities that an online environment can provide. Radically changing the packaging approach taken makes little sense when a great deal of effort has been spent over a number of years to develop and hone branded packaging into a sophisticated and highly developed communication. Randall Frost, in an article entitled 'Virtual packaging lacks sense', claims that strong packaging promotes confidence in a brand and that a consumer's tactile encounter with a package contributes to that experience. While a consumer cannot necessarily handle a product from an Internet store prior to purchase, this tactile element comes into play when the product is received, thereby reinforcing positive feelings towards the brand. Even though most packaging design for online compatibility will essentially consist of making adjustments to traditional packaging, some aspects of the process do need to be carefully thought through.

Displaying packaging online

Designers need to consider how a product will be shown or rendered in the online environment. In a store, a consumer sees the product at full-size and can handle it. Online, only an image of a product can be shown and this will almost certainly not be life size. When displayed small, the branded graphics on an online product become almost 'impotent', according to Herbert M Meyers, co-author of *The Visionary Package*. So how well will a reduced-size image of a product convey the carefully crafted brand message?

Packaging design for online products needs to be designed to create a strong visual impact when displayed in an online store, even at relatively small sizes. As the online environment operates differently, there is a valid argument for developing different approaches to traditional methods in order to take full advantage of the opportunities presented by new media.

Distribution of online goods

Products sold online still have to withstand the rigours of physical distribution by the postal service or a parcel courier. Products may require an additional outer sleeve or even to be boxed and stuffed with tissue paper; shredded paper or packing peanuts may also be necessary. Packaging a product well provides a company with the opportunity to show customers that it cares about how the product arrives and presents the designer with the additional challenge of extending the brand communication to the outer packaging. Think outside of the box by adding the logo, brand name and website on the outside of the box, parcel or packaging.

Good packaging can go some way to generating repeat sales and can wow people when the product arrives at their door. This is important as branding is still crucially significant for online retailers. For products sold online, it is important to make clear how consumers can receive after-sales service in the event of a potential product defect, either in the packaging itself or in the information contained within it.

Online marketing channels may provide many benefits and cost savings but they do not obviate the importance of communication and brand building. Sending products presents an opportunity to provide additional brand and product information via other communication pieces directly targeted at the consumer; for example, by including information and coupons for other products within the range. Adding a little something extra can help to create brand loyalty. However, individual packaging can also add significantly to the cost of shipping, and so a balance between adequate protection and economy must be struck.

Retail is moving away from traditional bricks-and-mortar stores to virtual spaces, such as the Internet, illustrated by the examples pictured here. The virtual mannequin (above) is an indicator of how people will commonly shop for clothes and other goods in the future. The web page for Jean Paul Gaultier perfumes (right) presents an online version of a boutique store, complete with concierge, stairway and rooms.

< Changing retail environments   **Environmental considerations**   Ethics of packaging >

Environmental considerations

Packaging is something physical that is produced from a wide range of raw materials, and so its production and disposal will have important environmental considerations, too. Consumers and manufacturers are increasingly concerned with the environmental impact of their actions. This has resulted in pressure on designers to rethink packaging design in order to minimise its environmental impact, while ensuring that it is still performing its protective and communication functions.

Sustainable packaging

The need to produce sustainable packaging has become more and more widespread as environmental awareness grows about the dangers of excessive production, consumption and the generation of waste. Packaging designers working for a wide range of sectors now seek to produce packaging that is environmentally sustainable and that will have little – or no – impact on the local or global ecosystem once it has exhausted its primary use.

    The sustainable packaging process looks at the raw materials used, at where they come from, and at how they will be disposed of at the end of the packaging's useful life. This process includes an evaluation of the 'carbon footprint' that the product will create. A carbon footprint refers to the total amount of greenhouse gas emissions that are produced by the packaging, and is often expressed in terms of the amount of carbon dioxide emitted. Once the size of the carbon footprint has been evaluated, a strategy can then be devised to successfully reduce it. This may be achieved by increasing the amount of recycled materials used and by reducing the amount of different materials or components employed to create the packaging, to make it easier to recycle or less harmful to dispose of. Using minimal packaging is a growing trend. Once a designer has conceived of the packaging design, it is routinely submitted to a life-cycle assessment.

Life-cycle assessment

This involves an investigation into and evaluation of the environmental impacts that will be caused by a given product, and gauges how that product measures up to the sustainability aims set by a company, including its likely impact on the whole of the supply chain. A key part of this process involves finding ways to change consumer behaviour by providing sufficient information that will enable users to make more informed decisions about choosing products that have sustainable packaging and which encourage them to recycle more.

Waste hierarchy

The term 'waste hierarchy' refers to waste management strategies based on the application of 'the three Rs' – reduce, reuse and recycle. The most desirable design strategy is to aim to reduce material usage, then to reuse materials and thirdly to recycle materials. At the very bottom of the hierarchy is the disposal of materials. This hierarchy can guide the decision-making process when creating sustainable packaging, in terms of materials' use, the size of container used and so on. For example, improving the protective attributes of an inner container may mean that outer packaging is no longer necessary (a prevention strategy) or that less is required (minimisation). Alternatively, the use of several types of plastic in a container could be reduced to one or two in order to make recycling easier (recycling).

The waste hierarchy diagram: this describes the most and least preferable options for dealing with waste that routinely arises from product packaging.

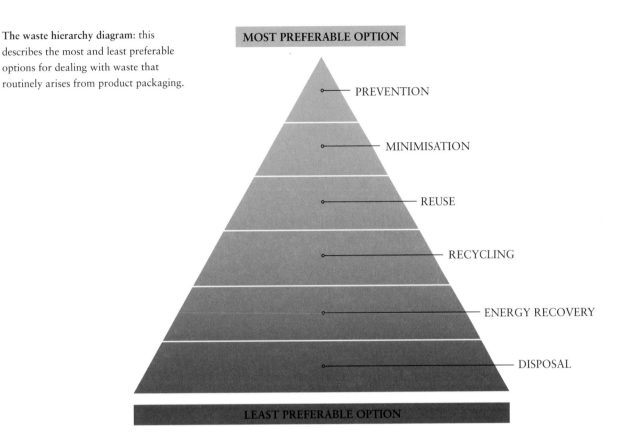

MOST PREFERABLE OPTION

PREVENTION

MINIMISATION

REUSE

RECYCLING

ENERGY RECOVERY

DISPOSAL

LEAST PREFERABLE OPTION

Creating packaging statements

Changing the packaging system used may result in considerable intervention and would likely require a rethink of all aspects of the packaging function. It may also, however, provide an opportunity to create a new packaging statement for a brand. For example, LUSH Fresh Handmade Cosmetics, a UK-based manufacturer and marketer of ethical beauty products, sells 65 per cent of its products 'naked' (that is, without packaging), while the rest have minimal packaging, including tissue paper, reusable tins and paper bags made from recycled materials. In 2007, it started using popcorn as loose-fill padding instead of shredded paper or polystyrene chips in its shipping package.

In practical terms, designers are largely seeking to produce packages that use fewer materials, to replace virgin raw materials with recycled materials and to simplify packaging designs so that they contain fewer different materials. The preferred strategy in the waste hierarchy is prevention, which requires only using packaging where it is absolutely needed. Proper packaging can prevent waste by preventing loss or damage to the contents of the package. Minimisation or source reduction seeks to reduce the mass and volume of packaging, which can also help reduce costs.

Reusing packaging

Packaging formats are gradually changing as increasing global environmental awareness among consumers and designers is causing dismay at the distance that products may have to travel and at the amount of packaging used to contain them. Retailers are consequently turning to focus on locally sourced produce and exploring ways to reduce packaging.

The development of new materials continues to change the packaging landscape by offering new ways to protect products, extend shelf life or maintain freshness for longer. Materials development also extends the possibilities available to designers to create packaging that fulfils branding requirements, such as better surfaced printability, films that can be colour printed or shrink-wrapped around containers and so on.

< Changing retail environments   **Environmental considerations**   Ethics of packaging >

IdeaPaint

Jones created this packaging for paint manufacturer IdeaPaint for its CRE-8 water-borne paint range (left), which uses a no-nonsense minimalist approach that reflects the straightforward environmental benefits of the product. Each label tells the consumer exactly what the product does; for example, each can of paint has sufficient material to cover 50 square feet of surface, which is the main message communicated by the label. IdeaPaint can turn virtually any surface into a dry-erase surface that allows people to write on their walls instead of using paper notes and is a product that uses fewer packaging and raw materials than traditional whiteboards.

'The blue and green colour palette evokes the purity of the water and the design of the packaging keeps waste to an absolute minimum.'

Wendy Thai, Ferroconcrete

echo

Ferroconcrete created the packaging pictured for the Los Angeles-based bottled water producer, echo (right). Echo wanted to design packaging that minimised its environmental impact. The bottle features a small label that is made from a quick-peel removable substrate so that consumers can easily peel it off and drop it in the recycling bin, along with the bottle, to aid the recycling process. The labels were printed in a carbon neutral, wind-powered facility to minimise the environmental impact of the energy used in their production. Echo assert that: 'Bottled water is just a convenience and we should be conscious of the impact each bottle has on the environment. Bottled water should be simple, local and responsibly packaged.'

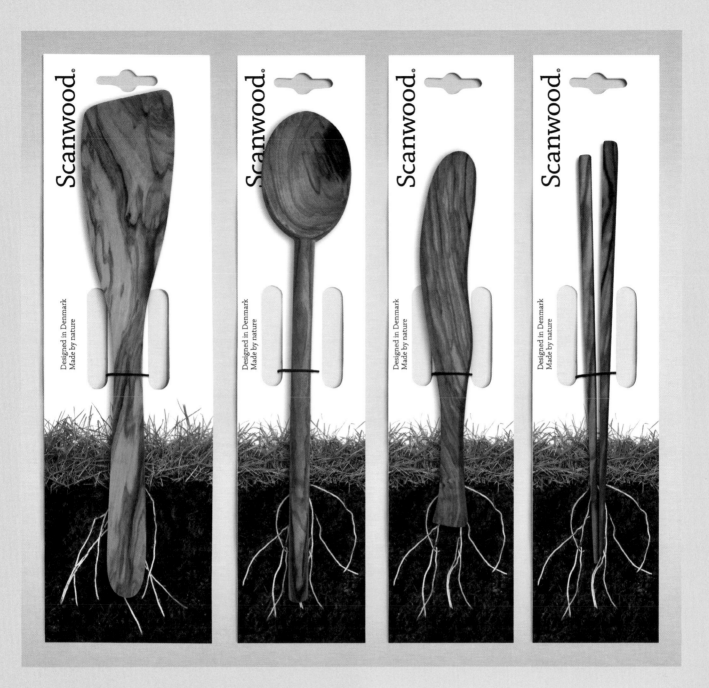

Scanwood

Danish designer Mads Jakob Poulsen created the packaging redesign for Scanwood, Denmark's largest manufacturer of wooden kitchenware, shown above. Scanwood wanted to communicate that its products are made through an environmentally friendly process and are made from all-natural materials. The design shows this visibly and implies that the product grows straight out of the ground, which combines with the tagline: 'Designed in Denmark, made by Nature'.

Speedo

The packaging redesign shown (right) was created by R Design for a range of Speedo swimming goggles. The company wanted to produce packaging that would be kinder to the environment, reduce costs and also increase the product's visual impact and shelf presence, so the design solution needed to consider structural form as much as the role of the graphics. The resultant packaging has saved 120 tons of PVC and 320 tons of plastic, which means that fewer chemicals are now used in the production process and less material ends up in landfill. The brand spread swiftly around the world and counts 300 products in its range that are sold in 14 different languages.

<u>Ethics of packaging</u>

Ethics are moral standards by which people judge behaviour. The ethics of packaging concerns both what packaging is made from and the statements that it makes about the product it contains – in other words, the behavioural ethos of the companies that make the products that we buy.

Global decisions

People are concerned about the environmental impact that their lives make. Products with excessive packaging or those that use non-renewable, non-recyclable or non-biodegradable materials are therefore increasingly viewed in a negative light. To make purchases that correspond with their ethical values, consumers require packaging to show the social, environmental and fair trade aspects of products, and want to know whether products may have damaging social consequences or may cause environmental harm in their place of origination. This may require an explicit statement from manufacturers about the ethical practices employed in creating a product or the use of certified symbols received by companies after undergoing a certification process.

Personal decisions

Each designer has their own personal ethical stance and opinions on prescient social issues, such as the environment and trade relations with developing countries. For example, not everyone is comfortable working for certain brands, organisations or products, such as the adult entertainment sector, or with cigarettes, alcohol, gambling or religion. At a certain point in their career, every packaging designer will face ethical questions contained in a design brief that may challenge or compromise their own personal beliefs – and will have to make the call about how best to respond to these implicit issues, or whether perhaps to ignore them altogether and deal with the consequences of this.

A Perfume Organic

Some packaging has a secondary function. The paper boxes pictured here are embedded with flower seeds and can be 'planted' after purchase. They are also printed with soy inks, reducing their impact on the environment. The company was established to offer a more ethically sound alternative to conventional perfumes, which typically use two groups of hazardous chemicals. Made from pure natural oils produced from USDA-certified organic materials, these scents are free from petrochemicals, solvents, dyes, pesticides and synthetic chemicals.

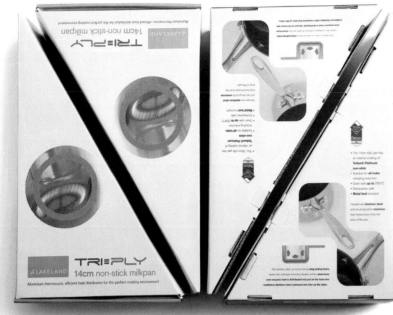

Lakeland

Nicepond created this minimalist triangular box packaging for Lakeland's tri-ply stainless steel pan range, which features photography of the pans in use. The triangle format grabs attention by virtue of its unusual presentation and reinforces the tri-ply nature of the product. The packaging uses less material than traditional boxes do, is stronger and allows more efficient use of space during transportation, and thus has significant environmental benefits, too.

the home of creative kitchenware™

< Ethics of packaging   **Case study**   Student exercise >

Case study

Good Ol' Sailor Vodka

Division

The Swedish design agency Division reinvented the vodka bottle for the Swedish Good Ol' Sailor brand of vodka, an environmentally friendly product. The vodka has been re-engineered and the brand reinvented to bring it up to date with the changing tastes and aspirations of the target audience. People are more concerned about their impact on the environment and want to use higher-quality and less-adulterated food and beverage products.

The product is one of the first made from organically grown, Swedish barley and it has been distilled four times (rather than double or triple distilled as for other vodkas) to give it a clean, fruity nose with some spicy aftertaste.

The high level of eco credentials of the product and its refinement meant that the designers had to create a bottle to suit. The designers chose to use Swedish-made PET packaging for minimal environmental impact through working closely with technologists at Petainer.

The resulting container is environmentally friendly, has high levels of clarity and great shelf appeal, whilst at the same time it is easy to manufacture in high volumes. 'We wanted to exploit the phenomenon of PET in the best possible way. The goal was to design packaging that would be integrated with the bottle' explain the designers. The reinvention of the product and the packaging also called for the reinvention of the brand and its graphics. The surface graphics of the bottle continued the nautical theme of the brand and were created by tattoo artist Mattias Brodén to give a highly distinctive and unmistakable visual message that really stands out from the shelf. 'What you notice first about Good Ol' Sailor Vodka is not the taste – but the bottle,' say the designers.

< Case study   **Student exercise**   Conclusion >

Student exercise

Ecological

Project set by Nigel Aono-Billson

The bottle created by Ferroconcrete for echo, a bottled water that was designed to have a minimal impact on the environment, has a 'quick-peel' removable label to enable quick and efficient recycling, and keeps wastage to an absolute minimum. The blue and green colour palette used is designed to allude to water purity. This design was previously discussed on page 188.

As designers, we have a responsibility to the environment, and to produce design work and creative solutions that have a minimal impact on the world around us. So much product packaging ends up as landfill, but by using sustainable, renewable materials for packaging production, both manufacturers and consumers can begin to be kinder to the environment and to the planet.

Being ecologically aware and choosing to use only materials such as paper and card, or plastics that are recyclable, compostable or biodegradable, all contributes to reducing the environmental impact of a given product and to raising social awareness of the need to do so. Moreover, paper and card are versatile materials, which can be cut, folded and moulded, allowing for almost limitless creative possibilities in terms of their shape, fabrication and manipulation.

Plastics, such as PET (polyethylene terephthalate, a thermoplastic polymer resin and a form of polyester) or RPET (recycled polyethylene terephthalate), can be used to make fibres for such things as carpet and fabric, sheet and film, or new PET for containers for both food and non-food products. Alternatively, recycled paper, vegetable-based materials, corn-starch bottles or edible packaging could form the base material for packaging or labelling design solutions.

Student exercise

Packaging a product with an ecological outcome

Packaging as a medium has a great global reach that touches billions of consumers every day. There is mounting concern, however, that producers and sellers are routinely over-packaging products. Do bananas, cucumbers and other such fruit and vegetables really need to be wrapped in plastic, for example? The over-usage of complicated and multi-layered packaging by most manufacturers is probably largely unnecessary in most instances.

Taking an ethical stance towards the environment can develop through adopting a thoughtful approach and attitude towards packaging design; along with an active desire to employ only the appropriate amounts and types of materials, which will naturally result in designs that have a minimal impact on the planet.

1. Create
Choose either a drink, a product or a food. Create a new piece of packaging that distinctly communicates the product's contents, and that is ethical and ecologically sound. The design must result in minimal environmental impact, must be competitive in its sector, and must convey the product message to consumers. Your challenge is to create unique packaging with a conscience. Look at all existing national and international brands with a similar proposition, and at retail outlets that could potentially stock the final product as a branded or own-label item.

2. Consider:
*   shape, form, size and quantities;
*   other similar products and brands;
*   record all similarities and dissimilarities;
*   individual packaging structures and materials.

3. Explore
*   Look at all existing global identities and brands.
*   The brand messages conveyed both on-pack and off-pack.
*   The size, shape and construction of all containers.
*   What the packaging is made from.
*   Whether the packaging is recycled or recyclable.
*   Whether the packaging is compostable or biodegradable.

Bibliography and further reading
Boylston, S. (2009). *Designing Sustainable Packaging*. Laurence King Publishing.

Imhoff, D. (2005). *Paper or Plastic: Searching for Solutions to an Overpackaged World*. Sierra Club Books.

Jedlicka, W. (2008). *Packaging Sustainability: Tools, Systems and Strategies for Innovative Package Design*. John Wiley & Sons.

Klanten, R. Ehmann, S. (2009). *Boxed and Labelled: New Approaches to Packaging Design*. Die Gestalten Verlag.

Sparke, P. (2010). *The Genius of Design*. Quadrille Publishing Ltd.

Conclusion

This book has discussed some of the main elements to consider when creating branded packaging for a product. It has shown that packaging performs many more functions than simply containing a product, and that packaging design can have a great impact in differentiating and ultimately achieving the goals of a brand.

Packaging, branding and design are changing. We are witnessing major cultural shifts as a consequence of the relentless process of globalisation – a smaller world, where we are all more familiar with certain products and brands. We are experiencing homogenization – where design styles are ironed out into a global language with less national variation. We are also going through a major change in buying habits, as online sales increase. All of these factors will go to affect the designs – and the designers – of the future, in ways that are not always easy to predict. But, hopefully, this book will have given you some basic principles that you can take forward into the emerging world of packaging design and that will help to inform your own design decisions as you shape tomorrow's design landscape.

Packaging the Brand has aimed to inspire you to think about packaging in different ways and to stimulate new ideas by showing examples of innovative contemporary packaging design solutions from leading designers and design agencies. We hope that it will continue to inspire you and help you to unlock your own creativity.

< Conclusion   **Contacts and credits**   Glossary of terms >

Contacts

Agency	Country	Website	Page No
1 Litre Water™	Canada	www.1litre.com	86
3 Deep Design	Australia	www.3deep.com.au	157, 169
Andy Vella	UK	www.velladesign.com	153, 165
A Perfume Organic	USA	www.aperfumeorganic.com	190
Bedow Creative	Sweden	www.bedow.se	68–69
Beetroot	Greece	www.beetroot.gr	80–81
Boy Bastiaens	The Netherlands	www.stormhand.com	inner page, 25, 166–167
burst*	UK	www.burst-design.com	19, 119, 151, 155, 160
BVD	Sweden	www.bvd.se	130–131
Colony	UK	www.colony.com	37
Contentismissing	Germany	www.contentismissing.net	125
Creative Orchestra	UK	www.creativeorchestra.com	62–63
Creasence	Czech Republic	www.creasence.com	79, 122, 168
Dan Alexander & Co	Tel Aviv and Paris	www.dgoldbergdesign.com	46, 170
DB Studio	UK	www.db-studio.co.uk	21, 33
DCA	UK	www.dca-design.com	59
Division	Sweden	www.thedivision.se	192–193
Ferroconcrete	USA	www.ferro-concrete.com	45, 188, 194
Flame	South Africa	www.flamedesign.co.za	25, 34
Freedom Of Creation	The Netherlands	www.freedomofcreation.com	142
GJP Advertising	Canada	www.gjpadvertising.com	103
GWORKSHOP	Ecuador	www.gworkshopdesign.com	171
Happy Forsman & Bodenfors	Sweden	www.happy.fb.se	87
Hatch	USA	www.hatchsf.com	29, 43, 148
Jones	USA	www.onesingfor.com	188
Lavernia & Cienfuegos	Spain	www.lavernia.com	83, 141, 161
Lewis Moberly	UK	www.lewismoberly.com	47, 75–77
lg2boutique	Canada	www.lg2boutique.com	120–121
Little Fury	USA	www.littlefury.com	72–73, 106, 153
Mads Jakob Poulsen	Denmark	www.madsjakobpoulsen.dk	189
Magnet Harlequin	UK	www.magharl.co.uk	71
Monnet Design	Canada	www.monnet.ca	176–77
Mookai	Canada	www.mookai.ca	139, 163
Mouse Graphics	Greece	www.mousegraphics.gr	99, 117, 118, 126, 159, 174
Neumeister	Sweden	www. neumeister.se	117, 161
Nicepond	UK	www.nicepond.com	191
Ogilvy & Mather	Germany	www.ogilvy.com	113
Pearlfisher	UK	www.pearlfisher.com	105, 156
Policarpo Design	Portugal	www.policarpodesign.com	39, 126
Prompt Design	Thailand	www.prompt-design.com	109
Propaganda	UK	www.propaganda.co.uk	17, 48–49
R Design	UK	www.r-design.co.uk	40, 100, 101, 104, 119, 154, 158
Reach	UK	www.reachbrands.co.uk	57, 66–67, 155, 189
Remo Caminada	Switzerland	www.remocaminada.com	110–111
Samal Design	Russia	www.samaldesign.com	143
Shane Cranford	USA	www.workingformorework.com	160
Stockholm Design Lab	Sweden	www.stockholmdesignlab.se	149
Strømme Throndsen Design	Norway	www.stdesign.no	36, 85, 123, 143
Studio Blackburn	UK	www.studioblackburn.com	71
Studio Kluif	The Netherlands	www.studiokluif.nl	127
The Experimental Project	Canada	www.theexperimentalproject.com	35
Thomas Manss & Company	UK	www.manss.com	168
Turner Duckworth	UK	www.turnerduckworth.com	36
Voice	Australia	www.voicedesign.net	88–91, 173
Wieden + Kennedy	USA	www.wk.com	36
Z3 Design Studio	UK	www.designbyz3.com	30–31, 124, 158

Credits

< Contacts and credits   **Glossary of terms**   Index >

Glossary of terms

Brand
A product, service or concept that is distinguished so that it can be effectively communicated and marketed.

Brand personality
The perceived personality of a brand that embodies key characteristics or aspects that the client wants to communicate to consumers, such as that the brand is safe, friendly, reliable or traditional.

Budget
The amount of money that is available to complete the design job. A budget will typically include a fee for the design agency, and production and distribution costs for the finished design.

Campaign
A series of coordinated activities to market and promote a brand. The packaging and brand design will form a central part of a campaign and so the designer must consider how it will be used and shown. Campaign activities could include print ads, TV spots and in-store promotions.

Carbon footprint
The total amount of greenhouse gas emissions caused by a product, often expressed in terms of the amount of carbon dioxide emitted. Once the size of a carbon footprint is known, a strategy can be devised to reduce it.

Channel
The distribution channels used to present a brand to the target market, including distribution points such as supermarkets, boutique stores and direct mail.

Consumer
The person that uses a product. Note that the consumer is not necessarily the buyer of a product.

Corporate colours
The specific colours that form the livery of a company or brand. Designers are often restricted in the colour palette they can choose from, because a brand or company may already have a suite of predetermined colours that it uses, typically specified by their Pantone numbers.

Corporate style sheet
The specific type and style of a company or brand. Designers will often be restricted in the typographic range that they can use because a brand or company will already have a predetermined style sheet that dictates the type styles that can be used, along with particular usage considerations.

Deadline
The date at which the design must be completed and delivered to the client, ready to use.

Deliverables
The actual items that the design agency will produce for the client, which may include a logo, a brand design, brand livery, packaging creation and so on.

ESP (emotional selling point)
A product selling point that makes an emotional appeal to the buyer.

Equity
The value of a brand, which in turn adds to the value of a product owing to the positive reaction that consumers have to it. Brand equity can become a significant USP in its own right.

FMCG
Fast moving consumer goods. These tend to be low-value, quick turn-around items.

Folk culture
Traditional modes of behaviour and expression transmitted from generation to generation among a group or people, the lifestyle of a culture passed on through oral tradition.

Franchise
A form of business in which a company with a successful product or service (the franchisor) establishes a business relationship with other people (franchisees), whereby the franchisee uses the franchisor's trade name, marketing and product offering in exchange for a fee.

Gondola
A retail merchandising display unit.

Gondola end or head
The end and most prized location of a retail merchandising display unit.

Identity
The collective characteristics by which a brand is recognised.

License
A legal permission to use a product, brand, name, patent or other concept for a specified period of time.

Licensee
The person or entity to whom the license is granted.

Licensor
The person or entity that grants the license.

Life-cycle assessment
The investigation and evaluation of the environmental impacts of a given product caused by its existence.

Livery
The distinctive colours in which a brand is presented.

Market position
The position in the market of the product and/or brand. A product may be a market leader, a market follower, a 'me-too' product, an own brand or a value product. The market position and aims of the client will inform development of the brand strategy.

Market research
A body of data collected from primary and secondary sources about a market segment, product type or consumer group.

Merchandise
A product or range of products.

Message
The message that the client wants to communicate through the brand will be the driving force and focus of the design. It is important that both the client and design agency are clear on their understanding of what the message at the centre of the design is.

Off the shelf
A product that is not custom-made and that is available from the merchandise carried in stock.

Outcomes
The anticipated results of the communication strategy of which the design will be part.

Project objectives
The ultimate aims of the design and the communication strategy it is part of. The objectives will affect how aggressive the communication strategy is and the brand design required to meet it.

Resolve
The design solution.

Royalty
A payment made for the use of property, especially a patent, copyrighted work, franchise or natural resource.

Shelf-edging strip
Marketing materials placed on the edge of a retail shelf, where shoppers look for price and size information.

Stock-keeping unit (SKU)
A unit that allows a product to be tracked for inventory purposes.

Structural packaging
Packaging that forms a supporting structure around a product.

Surface graphics
The graphics on the surface of packaging.

Target market
Who the product is aimed at. The target market will affect the brand strategies used, including language, typography, colour, style and image usage.

Typical consumer profile
A profile of the target consumer or consumer group that includes demographic information, such as age, sex, socio-economic group and so on. It can also include hypothetical information such as favourite food, drink, holiday location, clothing style, car and other information that completes the picture of who the target consumer is and what motivates them.

USP (unique selling point)
The main advantage or attraction of a product that can be featured in the design and communication, and which allows it to be differentiated. The USP has to be credible and believable by the target audience.

< Glossary of terms **Index** Acknowledgements >

Index

< Index   **Acknowledgements**   Working with ethics >

Acknowledgements

We would like to thank everyone who supported us during the project – the many art directors, designers and creatives who showed great generosity in allowing us to reproduce their work. Special thanks to everyone who hunted for, collated, compiled and rediscovered some of the fascinating work contained in this book. A special thanks to Boy Bastiaens for supplying the inside cover pages.

Thanks to Xavier Young for his patience, determination and skill in photographing the work showcased.

And a final big thanks to Colette Meacher, Brian Morris, Caroline Walmsley and all the staff at AVA Publishing who never tired of our requests, enquiries and questions, and supported us throughout.

Publisher's note

The subject of ethics is not new, yet its consideration within the applied visual arts is perhaps not as prevalent as it might be. Our aim here is to help a new generation of students, educators and practitioners find a methodology for structuring their thoughts and reflections in this vital area.

AVA Publishing hopes that these **Working with ethics** pages provide a platform for consideration and a flexible method for incorporating ethical concerns in the work of educators, students and professionals. Our approach consists of four parts:

The **introduction** is intended to be an accessible snapshot of the ethical landscape, both in terms of historical development and current dominant themes.

A selection of **further reading** for you to consider areas of particular interest in more detail.

The **framework** positions ethical consideration into four areas and poses questions about the practical implications that might occur. Marking your response to each of these questions on the scale shown will allow your reactions to be further explored by comparison.

The **case study** sets out a real project and then poses some ethical questions for further consideration. This is a focus point for a debate rather than a critical analysis so there are no predetermined right or wrong answers.

Required Reading Range
Working with ethics

Lynne Elvins
Naomi Goulder

Ethical: awareness/ reflection/ debate

Introduction

Ethics is a complex subject that interlaces the idea of responsibilities to society with a wide range of considerations relevant to the character and happiness of the individual. It concerns virtues of compassion, loyalty and strength, but also of confidence, imagination, humour and optimism. As introduced in ancient Greek philosophy, the fundamental ethical question is: *what should I do?* How we might pursue a 'good' life not only raises moral concerns about the effects of our actions on others, but also personal concerns about our own integrity.

In modern times the most important and controversial questions in ethics have been the moral ones. With growing populations and improvements in mobility and communications, it is not surprising that considerations about how to structure our lives together on the planet should come to the forefront. For visual artists and communicators, it should be no surprise that these considerations will enter into the creative process.

Some ethical considerations are already enshrined in government laws and regulations or in professional codes of conduct. For example, plagiarism and breaches of confidentiality can be punishable offences. Legislation in various nations makes it unlawful to exclude people with disabilities from accessing information or spaces. The trade of ivory as a material has been banned in many countries. In these cases, a clear line has been drawn under what is unacceptable.

But most ethical matters remain open to debate, among experts and lay-people alike, and in the end we have to make our own choices on the basis of our own guiding principles or values. Is it more ethical to work for a charity than for a commercial company? Is it unethical to create something that others find ugly or offensive?

Specific questions such as these may lead to other questions that are more abstract. For example, is it only effects on humans (and what they care about) that are important, or might effects on the natural world require attention too?

Is promoting ethical consequences justified even when it requires ethical sacrifices along the way? Must there be a single unifying theory of ethics (such as the Utilitarian thesis that the right course of action is always the one that leads to the greatest happiness of the greatest number), or might there always be many different ethical values that pull a person in various directions?

As we enter into ethical debate and engage with these dilemmas on a personal and professional level, we may change our views or change our view of others. The real test though is whether, as we reflect on these matters, we change the way we act as well as the way we think. Socrates, the 'father' of philosophy, proposed that people will naturally do 'good' if they know what is right. But this point might only lead us to yet another question: *how do we know what is right?*

Further reading

AIGA
Design Business and Ethics
2007, AIGA

Eaton, Marcia Muelder
Aesthetics and the Good Life
1989, Associated University Press

Ellison, David
Ethics and Aesthetics in European Modernist Literature:
From the Sublime to the Uncanny
2001, Cambridge University Press

Fenner, David E W (Ed)
Ethics and the Arts:
An Anthology
1995, Garland Reference Library of Social Science

Gini, Al and Marcoux, Alexei M
Case Studies in Business Ethics
2005, Prentice Hall

McDonough, William and Braungart, Michael
Cradle to Cradle:
Remaking the Way We Make Things
2002, North Point Press

Papanek, Victor
Design for the Real World:
Making to Measure
1972, Thames & Hudson

United Nations Global Compact
The Ten Principles
www.unglobalcompact.org/AboutTheGC/
TheTenPrinciples/index.html

A framework for ethics

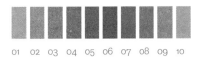

Your specifications
What are the impacts of your materials?

In relatively recent times, we are learning that many natural materials are in short supply. At the same time, we are increasingly aware that some man-made materials can have harmful, long-term effects on people or the planet. How much do you know about the materials that you use? Do you know where they come from, how far they travel and under what conditions they are obtained? When your creation is no longer needed, will it be easy and safe to recycle? Will it disappear without a trace? Are these considerations your responsibility or are they out of your hands?

Using the scale, mark how ethical your material choices are.

You
What are your ethical beliefs?

Central to everything you do will be your attitude to people and issues around you. For some people, their ethics are an active part of the decisions they make every day as a consumer, a voter or a working professional. Others may think about ethics very little and yet this does not automatically make them unethical. Personal beliefs, lifestyle, politics, nationality, religion, gender, class or education can all influence your ethical viewpoint.

Using the scale, where would you place yourself? What do you take into account to make your decision? Compare results with your friends or colleagues.

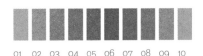

Your creation
What is the purpose of your work?

Between you, your colleagues and an agreed brief, what will your creation achieve? What purpose will it have in society and will it make a positive contribution? Should your work result in more than commercial success or industry awards? Might your creation help save lives, educate, protect or inspire? Form and function are two established aspects of judging a creation, but there is little consensus on the obligations of visual artists and communicators toward society, or the role they might have in solving social or environmental problems. If you want recognition for being the creator, how responsible are you for what you create and where might that responsibility end?

Using the scale, mark how ethical the purpose of your work is.

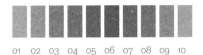

Your client
What are your terms?

Working relationships are central to whether ethics can be embedded into a project, and your conduct on a day-to-day basis is a demonstration of your professional ethics. The decision with the biggest impact is whom you choose to work with in the first place. Cigarette companies or arms traders are often-cited examples when talking about where a line might be drawn, but rarely are real situations so extreme. At what point might you turn down a project on ethical grounds and how much does the reality of having to earn a living affect your ability to choose?

Using the scale, where would you place a project? How does this compare to your personal ethical level?

Case study

One aspect of graphic design that raises an ethical dilemma is that of its relationship with the creation of printed materials and the environmental impacts of print production. For example, in the UK, it is estimated that around 5.4 billion items of addressed direct mail are sent out every year and these, along with other promotional inserts, amount to over half a million tonnes of paper annually (almost 5 per cent of the UK consumption of paper and board). Response rates to mail campaigns are known to be between 1–3 per cent, making junk mail arguably one of the least environmentally friendly forms of print communication. As well as the use of paper or board, the design decisions to use scratch-off panels, heavily coated gloss finishes, full-colour ink-intensive graphics or glues for seals or fixings make paper more difficult to recycle once it has been discarded. How much responsibility should a graphic designer have in this situation if a client has already chosen to embark on a direct mail campaign and has a format in mind? Even if designers wish to minimise the environmental impacts of print materials, what might they most usefully do?

Is it more ethical to create promotional graphics for 'healthy' rather than 'unhealthy' food products?

Is it unethical to design cartoon characters to appeal to children for commercial purposes?

Would you have worked on this project, either now or in the 1950s?

I studied graphic design in Germany, and my professor emphasised the responsibility that designers and illustrators have towards the people they create things for.

Eric Carle
(illustrator)

Tony the Tiger

In 1951, Leo Burnett (the famous advertising executive known for creating the Jolly Green Giant and the Marlboro Man) was hired to create a campaign for Kellogg's new cereal, Sugar Frosted Flakes (now Frosties in the UK and Frosted Flakes in the US). Tony the Tiger, designed by children's book illustrator Martin Provensen, was one of four characters selected to sell the cereal. Newt the Gnu and Elmo the Elephant never made it to the shelves and after Tony proved more popular than Katy the Kangaroo, she was dropped from packs after the first year.

Whilst the orange-and-black tiger stripes and the red kerchief have remained, Provensen's original design for Tony has changed significantly since he first appeared in 1952. Tony started out with an American football-shaped head, which later became more rounded, and his eye colour changed from green to gold. Today, his head is more angular and he sits on a predominantly blue background. Tony was initially presented as a character that walked on all fours and was no bigger than a cereal box. By the 1970s, Tony's physique had developed into a slim and muscular six-foot-tall standing figure.

Between 1952 and 1995 Kellogg's are said to have spent more than USD$1 billion promoting Frosted Flakes with Tony's image, while generating USD$5.3 billion in gross US sales. But surveys by consumer rights groups such as Which? find that over 75 per cent of people believe that using characters on packaging makes it hard for parents to say no to their children. In these surveys, Kellogg's come under specific scrutiny for Frosties, which are said to contain one third sugar and more salt than the Food Standards Agency recommends. In response, Kellogg's have said: 'We are committed to responsibly marketing our brands and communicating their intrinsic qualities so that our customers can make informed choices.'

Food campaigners claim that the use of cartoon characters is a particularly manipulative part of the problem and governments should stop them being used on less healthy children's foods. But in 2008, spokespeople for the Food and Drink Federation in the UK, said: 'We are baffled as to why Which? wants to take all the fun out of food by banning popular brand characters, many of whom have been adding colour to supermarket shelves for more than 80 years.'